Revising U.S.Military Strategy

Pergamon Titles of Related Interest

Revising U.S.Military Strategy
Tailoring Means to Ends

Jeffrey Record

Institute for Foreign Policy Analysis, Inc.

Published in cooperation with the
Institute for Foreign Policy Analysis, Inc.

PERGAMON·BRASSEY'S
International Defense Publishers

Washington New York Oxford Toronto Sydney Paris Frankfurt

Pergamon Press Offices:

U.S.A.   Pergamon-Brassey's International Defense Publishers,
1340 Old Chain Bridge Road, McLean, Virginia, 22101, U.S.A

Pergamon Press Inc., Maxwell House, Fairview Park,
Elmsford, New York 10523, U.S.A.

U.K.   Pergamon Press Ltd., Headington Hill Hall,
Oxford OX3 0BW, England

CANADA   Pergamon Press Canada Ltd., Suite 104, 150 Consumers Road,
Willowdale, Ontario M2J 1P9, Canada

AUSTRALIA   Pergamon Press (Aust.) Pty. Ltd., P.O. Box 544,
Potts Point, NSW 2011, Australia

FRANCE   Pergamon Press SARL, 24 rue des Ecoles,
75240 Paris, Cedex 05, France

FEDERAL REPUBLIC Pergamon Press GmbH, Hammerweg 6,
OF GERMANY   D-6242 Kronberg-Taunus, Federal Republic of Germany

Copyright © 1984 Pergamon - Brassey's International Defense Publishers

Library of Congress Cataloging in Publication Data

Record, Jeffrey.
    Revising U.S. military strategy.

    Bibliography: p.
    Includes index.
    1. United States--Military policy. 2. Strategy.
I. Title. II. Title: Revising US military strategy.
UA23.R36 1984   355'.0335'73   84-9228
ISBN 0-08-031619-0
ISBN 0-08-031618-2 (pbk.)

Printed in the United States of America

CONTENTS

Revising U.S.Military Strategy

INTRODUCTION

The late Sir Basil Liddell Hart defined military strategy as "the art of distributing and applying military means to fulfill the ends of policy."[1] Hart went on to note that

> . . . strategy depends for success, first and most, on a sound *calculation and co-ordination of the ends and the means*. The end must be proportioned to the total means, and the means used in gaining each intermediate end which contributes to the ultimate must be proportioned to the value and needs of that intermediate end—whether it be to gain an objective or to fulfill a contributory purpose.[2]

Writing a quarter of a century earlier, Edward Mead Earle defined strategy as "the art of controlling and utilizing the resources of a nation—or a coalition of nations—including its armed forces, to the end that its vital interests shall be effectively promoted and secured against enemies, actual, potential, or merely presumed."[3] Although Earle's definition is really that of *grand* strategy (encompassing nonmilitary as well as military resources), it captures the essence of strategy at any level—namely, the tailoring of goals to resources within a specific internal and external political, military, and economic environment.

Strategy is the calculated relationship of purpose and power. It involves choices within a framework of finite resources, and an ability to distinguish between the desirable and the possible, the essential and the expendable. A sound sense of priorities is the essence of sound strategy. When the United States entered World War II, it pursued a "Germany first" strategy, concentrating the main weight of its military effort against the most powerful and dangerous member of the Axis, while initially remaining on the strategic defensive in the Pacific. History has confirmed the wisdom of that strategy, although it entailed some hard choices early in the war against Japan, including the decision to write off the Philippines.

A strategy whose goals far exceed resources available for their implementation is a recipe for potential disaster. The same may be said of a strategy that fails to adapt effectively to fundamental changes in the national and international political, military, and economic environment. Thus the Third Reich ultimately was doomed by the abyss that separated Hitler's virtually unlimited military objectives in Europe and the actual military resources available to fulfill them. Thus the failure of French strategy in the 1930s to adapt effectively to the military

1

consequences of the Munich agreement of 1938, and to such unfolding new military technologies as the tank and the airplane, contributed decisively to France's swift defeat in 1940.

To be sure, one must be ever mindful of Clausewitz's distinction between "preparations for war" and "war proper,"[4] a distinction similar, but not identical, to that in contemporary Western military parlance between "deterrence" and "defense." Planning for war—even for the explicit purpose of averting it (deterrence)—is not the same as waging war, and the ultimate test of any military strategy is not whether it succeeds in maintaining peace but whether, in the event of war, it can restore peace on politically favorable terms and at an acceptable cost. This is another way of saying that deterrence and defense are inseparable— that the ability, actual or perceived, to wage war successfully is the best means of avoiding the necessity to wage it at all.

Unfortunately, what has passed for American military strategy during the past two decades has all too often amounted to little more than periodic professions of military desire undisciplined either by a realistic appreciation of the finite limits of U.S. military power or by effective accommodation to fundamental changes in the global geostrategic environment. To be sure, since 1945 there has always been a significant gap between declared U.S. military goals and actual capabilities to fulfill them. The United States in the postwar era has never possessed military power sufficient to deliver on all its defense commitments overseas, and certainly not simultaneously. Realization of stated goals for a "2½-war" and even a "1½-war" capability has consistently eluded the Pentagon, which had to dig deeply into forces withheld in the United States as a strategic reserve in order to sustain the unexpectedly long and demanding "½-war" in Vietnam. This strategy/force mismatch, however, was tolerable in an era in which the United States enjoyed pronounced nuclear superiority, dominated the world's oceans, and faced no potential adversary perceived to be capable of mounting concurrent, decisive assaults on vital American interests in more than one region of the world.

Today's global geostrategic environment is much less favorable than that of the 1950s and early 1960s. During the past twenty years U.S. military power has sharply declined relative to that of the Soviet Union, which is now capable of sustaining a global conflict on more than one front. America's nuclear superiority has vanished, as has its unchallenged control of the seas. The locus and character of the Soviet threat to the West has moreover evolved far beyond that of a direct assault in Europe.

To make matters worse, the relative decline in American military power has been accompanied by an expansion in U.S. military obligations abroad. Large and exceedingly demanding commitments in the greater Persian Gulf area (Southwest Asia) have been added to traditional U.S. military commitments in Europe and East Asia in the absence of any significant expansion in U.S. force levels. The result has been a widening divergence between U.S. military responsibilities and resources.

The problem inherent in achieving a "sound calculation and coordination of . . . ends and . . . means" is reflected in Secretary of Defense Caspar W. Weinberger's *Annual Report to the Congress for Fiscal Year 1984*:

> Our long-term goal is to be able to meet the demands of a worldwide war, including concurrent reinforcement of Europe, deployments to Southwest Asia and the Pacific, and support for other areas. . . .
>
> Given the Soviets' capability to launch simultaneous attacks in [Southwest Asia], NATO, and the Pacific, our long-range goal is to be capable of defending all theaters simultaneously.[5]

Although the desirability of being "able to meet the demands of a worldwide war" is not at issue, there remains the question of America's *capacity* to do so. Aside from the fact that Soviet strategic interests in a worldwide conflict might not be well served by simultaneous attacks on two or more geographically separate fronts (the preferred alternative might be sequential assaults—for example, an initial strategic feint in Southwest Asia, aimed at drawing U.S. military resources away from Europe, where a subsequent and decisive blow would then be launched), "defending all [three] theaters simultaneously" is simply beyond the present and anticipated military resources of the United States. A "three-front" war against a numerically superior adversary enjoying the advantages of internal lines of communication (although not with respect to the Far East, which is logistically "closer" to the western coast of the United States than it is to the industrial and military heartland of the Soviet Union), could lead to a dangerous dispersion of U.S. forces in the face of a larger and more compact opponent. As Frederick the Great once observed, "He who attempts to defend too much defends nothing."[6]

Members of the Joint Chiefs of Staff have conceded the existence of a perilously widening gap between defense commitments and capabilities. In close questioning before the Senate Armed Services Committee in February 1982, then-Army Chief of Staff General Edward C. Meyer stated that "we are accepting tremendous risks with the size of forces that we have to do what we have pledged to do."[7] In their annual posture statement for fiscal year 1984 the Joint Chiefs stated that

> . . . with regard to these global responsibilities, U.S. forces are obviously not available to defend everywhere against every threat at all times. . . . Because our current forces are insufficient to take on all tasks simultaneously, general strategic priorities and the specific circumstances and forces available at the time will govern force employment.[8]

To its credit, the Reagan Administration has recognized the "tremendous risks" inherent in the gap between U.S. military obligations and capabilities that it inherited in 1981 and has sought to narrow that gap via a major military build-up aimed at reversing the unfortunate defense investment trends of the 1970s. All three "legs" of the U.S. intercontinental nuclear deterrent are to be modernized; the U.S. Fleet is to be expanded from 423 combatants (in 1981) to over 600; significant increases in strategic sea- and airlift capabilities are under way; and the readiness and weaponry of the U.S. Army and Air Force are being substantially upgraded. Moreover, despite its ongoing public commitment to "defending all theaters simultaneously," the Administration in 1982 conceded that a global war with the Soviet Union would dictate sequential U.S. military operations based on a combination of strategic priorities and operational opportunities.

Whether the administration's military program will bring even sequentially serviced U.S. military obligations and power into line remains to be seen, however. In testimony before the Senate Armed Services Committee, Undersecretary of Defense Fred Iklé admitted that "even an increase in U.S. military investments as high as 14 percent per year [in real terms], continued throughout the decade, would not close the gap in accumulated military assets between the United States and the Soviet Union until the early 1990s." Iklé went on to conclude that "that is a bleak outlook, implying . . . a need for a defense increase considerably steeper than what the administration now proposes."[9] This "bleak outlook" certainly is not lessened by the conclusion of a growing number of defense analysts that the Pentagon is institutionally incapable of translating even a massive increase in defense spending into anything approaching a commensurate expansion of fighting power. A 1982 analysis sponsored by the Heritage Foundation concluded that unrealistic cost planning and force development decisions are not only endemic within the Department of Defense, but also will rob the Reagan Administration of much of the force increases anticipated under its Five-Year Defense Plan.[10]

To be sure, the United States and her allies did prevail simultaneously on two independent fronts during World War II. It should be recalled, however, that it took four years and a level of defense expenditure that at one point approached 40 percent of the gross national product to achieve victory. As former Chairman of the Joint Chiefs of Staff General David C. Jones has observed, "we had the time and the geographic isolation to mobilize American industry,"[11] two commodities that probably will not be available to the United States in a future conflict with the Soviet Union.

It also should be recalled that victory in Europe, the primary front, would have been impossible without the assistance of two other world powers, one of whose efforts alone accounted for the destruction of well over one-half of Germany's military forces. In the event of another global conflict, the vast industrial and human resources of one of those powers, the Soviet Union, will be arrayed *against* the United States; and the relative military weight of the other, Great Britain, has dwindled drastically since 1945.

Indeed, no discussion of past, present, or future U.S. military strategy can ignore America's historic and continuing dependence on powerful allies as a means of fulfilling its own national military objectives in both peace and war. Coalition warfare has been the hallmark of American security and military success in the twentieth century, as it was for Great Britain from the rise of Napoleon to the fall of the Third Reich. The necessity for coalition warfare cannot be emphasized enough. The United States alone has never conducted successful major operations on the Eurasian landmass; such ventures have always been undertaken in conjunction with numerically superior land forces of local allies.

It is in regard to coalition warfare that one can identify one of the two consistently favorable trends in the geostrategic environment since the early 1960s (the other being the disintegration of the Sino-Soviet alliance). Although U.S. military power has steadily declined relative to that of the Soviet Union, the collective real and potential military power of America's European and East Asian allies has risen. Until the late 1950s, most NATO and East Asian allies were still recovering from World War II, and much of the military power they possessed was being sapped in fruitless attempts to hang on to disintegrating colonial empires. Their relative military weight in the East–West strategic calculus was small. Today, the United States enjoys in Europe and Northeast Asia a network of allies whose collective economic power and standing conventional military forces far exceed our own, although few devote as much of their national wealth to defense as does the United States. Thus the decline in U.S. military power in relation to that of the Soviet Union has been in some measure offset by the relative rise in allied economic and potential military power vis-à-vis the United States.

When all is said and done, there appear to be four paths to achieving a reasonable congruency of U.S. military obligations and power. These paths are not mutually exclusive. The first would be simply to expand U.S. force levels to the point where they would be "able to meet the demands of a worldwide war, including concurrent reinforcement of Europe, deployments to Southwest Asia and the Pacific, and support for other areas." This solution, however, may not be feasible. As noted, even the Reagan Administration's military program (which, it is to be noted in passing, calls for levels of defense expenditure, as a percentage both of federal spending and of the gross national product, well below those of the peacetime years of Eisenhower's administrations) may fall short of meeting the force requirements of the Administration's announced strategy. Nor can full realization of the Administration's military program be taken for granted. The public and Congressional consensus on defense that began to emerge in 1979–1980, and which sustained the Reagan defense program in 1981–1982, is showing signs of weakening under the weight of unprecedented federal deficits, despite promising signs of major economic recovery in 1983. Political reaction to what many regard as excessive defense spending was evident in 1983 when the Congress voted to slash in half the 10.5 percent real spending increase proposed in the fiscal 1984 defense budget. Force expansion, in short, does not appear to be a fiscally or politically realistic solution to the mismatch between strategy and power.

A second solution would be to reduce U.S. defense commitments overseas to a level sustainable by existing U.S. forces, a solution that has been advanced by some neoisolationists and antimilitary liberals, and by those angered by allies perceived to be unwilling to bear their fair share of the common military burden. The problem with this solution is that a reduction in U.S. overseas commitments sufficient to bring U.S. military obligations strictly into line with current force levels would compel abandonment of critical treaty allies in both Europe and East Asia, which in turn could spark a pell-mell rush on their part to accommodate the Soviet Union in a manner disastrous to the security interests of the United States itself. Notwithstanding its nostalgic appeal to some Americans, Fortress America is no longer a politically or militarily viable concept in an age of intercontinental ballistic missiles and global economic interdependence.

A third solution would be to squeeze more fighting power out of existing U.S. forces by changing the way the Pentagon does business. This is the preferred course of the military reform movement and others who are persuaded that the real problems facing the U.S. military stem not from lack of resources but from institutional, doctrinal, and hardware design deficiencies that severely inhibit translation of expanded defense investment into commensurate increases in combat power. Prominent among these deficiencies, according to the reformers, are: a highly centralized personnel management system, which, by continually shuffling officers and men from unit to unit and job to job, produces low levels of unit cohesion on the battlefield; continued allegiance to attrition-oriented operational doctrines against a potential adversary capable of inflicting and absorbing greater losses than U.S. forces; and a weapons design philosophy and procurement procedures that produce unnecessarily complex and costly weapons that cannot be bought in sufficient numbers or properly maintained.

Prospects for fundamental military reform do not, however, seem promising. Many of the conclusions of the reform critique are far from self-evident; and with the exception of the U.S. Army, which has adopted a new, maneuver-oriented operational doctrine and is testing a New Manning System designed to promote unit cohesion, the armed services, for the most part, are not sympathetic to the claims and proposals of the reformers.

A fourth solution lies in a new division of military labor within the West as a whole, along both functional and geographic lines and entailing allied assumption of greater responsibility for tasks heretofore borne largely or disproportionately by the United States. This solution is predicated on the twin convictions that our European and East Asian allies, now fully recovered from World War II and possessed of human and economic resources far surpassing those of the United States, can and ought to bear a significantly larger share of the common military burden; and that the virtues of military specialization inherent in the differing military capabilities and geographic positions of the United States and its major allies can and ought to be exploited to a far greater extent than they have been to date.

The essence of the solution would be a level of allied military power commensurate with allied economic power coupled with expanded allied self-defense efforts that would serve to release U.S. military power for the defense of shared interests in logistically remote areas of the world—for example, Southwest Asia—beyond the effective military reach of most allies.

A precedent for such a new division of military labor, at least along functional lines, exists in the Guam Doctrine, proclaimed by President Nixon in 1969. In anticipation of post-Vietnam cuts in U.S. military power, the Guam Doctrine placed upon U.S. Asian allies the primary responsibility for their own defense on the ground, restricting the U.S. contribution largely to the provision of naval and air power and, where needed, logistical support. Paradoxically, the doctrine is, if anything, more applicable to Europe and Northeast Asia today than it ever was in Southeast Asia. The quality of European, Korean, and Japanese ground forces is much higher than was South Vietnam's, and NATO governments, as well as those of Korea and Japan, are far more economically capable of sustaining the material requirements of land warfare.

The principal obstacles to such a new division of military labor are, of course, allied political resistance to increased defense spending and allied fears that doing more for themselves might lead to a weakening of the U.S. commitment to their security. These obstacles, however, are not insurmountable. There is much that our allies can do to enhance their military capabilities at relatively low cost, such as increasing the operational effectiveness of their vast pool of trained manpower no longer on active duty and eliminating unnecessarily redundant investment in certain weapons and types of military forces. Allied apprehension that a diminished U.S. force presence on their territory could lead to a diminished U.S. commitment to their defense could be assuaged through a carefully discriminating, consultative approach to the entire issue and realization of the new division of military labor in carefully calibrated stages over a period of years.

U.S. allies must be firmly encouraged to do more for their own defense, if for no other reason than to thwart mounting public and Congressional pressures for unilateral withdrawals of U.S. troops stationed in Europe and elsewhere overseas. Even were such pressures not a factor, however, a compelling case can be made, on geostrategic grounds alone, for a new functional and geographic division of military labor among the United States and its allies.

Such a new division of military labor within NATO, especially if reinforced by other initiatives including a more intimate U.S. strategic engagement of China and greater U.S. investment in strategic mobility and ready reserve forces, would go a long way toward harmonizing U.S. (and Western) military ends and means.

The purpose of this study is to explore means of bridging the gap between U.S. military aspirations and resources within the framework both of history and of recent trends in the global geostrategic environment. The study focuses on strategy, not grand strategy, and rests on the premise that a *reasonable* harmony of ends and means is the essence of a sound strategy. Some measure of discrepancy—usually significant—between military objectives and capabilities is characteristic of most powers. Few states maintain standing forces in peacetime sufficient to wage major war. Even the Soviet Union would be compelled to call up reserves, mobilize industry, and commandeer nonmilitary transportation in the event of war. For the United States such a mismatch is inevitable, especially in light of the vast growth of Soviet military power during the past decade. A modest mismatch is also tolerable—even economically desirable—in peacetime, especially if force planning reflects a clear sense of strategic priorities and is predicated on sequential rather than simultaneous engagement of the designated threat. The present disparity between U.S. military ends and means, however, exceeds even the most generous definition of "modest," and U.S. force planning, as will be seen, has yet to accommodate that disparity.

The study also focuses on conventional deterrence and defense, with particular emphasis on the U.S.–European military relationship. The present nuclear stalemate between the United States and the Soviet Union is likely to persist indefinitely, and the defense of Europe remains the single most important determinant of the size and structure of U.S. conventional forces. NATO Europe, moreover, collectively possesses the largest ground and tactical air forces available to the West. Finally, the study focuses on ideas and concepts; the aim is to provide food for thoughtful and constructive discussion of fundamental issues confronting the Western Alliance.

The study does not attempt to assess in detail the political feasibility of proposed alterations in U.S. and allied military posture with respect either to domestic constraints or to relationships among allies. The political obstacles to realization of many of the ideas advanced in this study are admittedly formidable, and NATO's record in solving politically sensitive military issues has not been an altogether encouraging one. For decades critical military problems facing the Alliance were either ignored or deemed comparatively unimportant against a backdrop of pronounced U.S. nuclear superiority. Today, many of those issues, such as the role of conventional defense in an era of nuclear stalemate and burden-sharing with respect to deterrence of threats to vital Western interests outside the NATO Treaty area, have acquired so acute a political sensitivity as to block any prospect of their satisfactory resolution in the absence of sustained statesmanship of the highest caliber. Our European and East Asian allies are no longer economic and military wards of the United States (the principal exception being Japan, whose status under the terms of the U.S.–Japanese Security Treaty remains that of a U.S. military protectorate); most are economically robust *and* militarily capable sovereign states possessing honest differences of opinion on important military questions.

The following five chapters trace and assess the evolution of declared U.S. military objectives from 1945 through the present, and the relationship between strategic aspirations and actual military power. Particular emphasis is accorded (in Chapter 4) to the period from 1979 to the present, which has witnessed a major inflation in U.S. military commitments abroad without commensurate increases in U.S. military power.

Chapter 5 identifies and analyzes the implications for U.S. and allied strategy of four profound changes in the geostrategic environment since the 1960s: the loss of U.S. nuclear supremacy and attendant decline in U.S. military power in relation to that of the Soviet Union; the shift in the locus and character of the Soviet military threat; the shift in the East–West maritime balance; and the overall rise in Europe's economic and potential military power in relation to that of the United States.

Chapters 6 through 10 propose and discuss new means of bringing U.S. military obligations and power into reasonable harmony. Those means include a new transatlantic division of military labor (Chapter 6); a more intimate strategic engagement of China (Chapter 7); application of Western military strengths against Soviet military weaknesses (Chapter 8); greater U.S. and allied reliance on reserve forces (Chapter 9); and accelerated U.S. investment in strategic mobility (Chapter 10).

The final chapter summarizes the conclusions of the study.

It should be noted that most of the ideas and concepts underlying the study's specific recommendations have for years been focal points of discussion and debate within the U.S. foreign policy and defense community, and that some (though by no means all) of the study's proposed alterations in U.S. force posture are, in some measure, already being pursued by the Reagan Administration. As will be evident, however, the author believes that much more needs to be done than is now being done to bring U.S. military responsibilities and resources into reasonable harmony.

NOTES

1. B. H. Liddell Hart, *Strategy* (New York: Frederick A. Praeger, 1967), p. 335.
2. Ibid. p. 336 (original italics).
3. Edward Meade Earle, ed., *Makers of Modern Strategy* (Princeton: Princeton University Press, 1943), p. viii.
4. Karl von Clausewitz, *On War*, edited and translated by Michael Howard and Peter Paret with Introductory Essays by Peter Paret, Michael Howard, and Bernard Brodie (Princeton: Princeton University Press, 1976), pp. 131–132.
5. Caspar W. Weinberger, *Annual Report to the Congress for Fiscal Year 1984* (Washington, D.C.: U.S. Government Printing Office, 1983), p. 209.
6. *Frederick the Great and the Art of War*, edited and translated by Jay Luvaas (New York: The Free Press, 1966), p. 120.
7. Edward C. Meyer, Hearing transcripts, February 2, 1982.
8. *United States Military Posture FY 1984* (Washington, D.C.: Department of Defense, 1983), p. 6.
9. Fred Iklé, Statement before the Senate Armed Services Committee, February 26, 1982, p. 3.
10. George W. S. Kuhn, "Ending Defense Stagnation," in Richard N. Holwill, ed., *Agenda '83* (Washington, D.C.: The Heritage Foundation, 1982), pp. 69–114.
11. David C. Jones, "What's Wrong With Our Defense Establishment," *New York Times Magazine* (November 7, 1982), p. 70.

PART I.
U.S. MILITARY ASPIRATIONS AND RESOURCES IN THE POSTWAR ERA

PART I.
U.S. MILITARY ASPIRATIONS AND RESOURCES IN THE POSTWAR ERA

U.S. military aspirations since World War II have reflected the fundamental objective of American foreign policy since the late 1940s: the containment of Communist expansion on the Eurasian landmass beyond those areas occupied by Soviet armed forces at the close of World War II. Those aspirations have evolved in concert with changing perceptions of the nature of Communist expansion and changing judgments as to the best means of thwarting it.

Military power has always been viewed as one of several means of containing Communist expansion; these have included diplomatic and economic initiatives, security assistance, covert action, psychological warfare, and arms control ventures. Military and nonmilitary instruments of containment often have been employed in conjunction with one another, and the relative importance accorded them has registered significant alterations from one period to another. In terms of where and how to frustrate Communist expansion, containment has at times been applied selectively, with an emphasis on nonmilitary measures; at other times, it has been applied indiscriminately, with a virtually exclusive reliance on force. The goal of containing Communist expansion, however, has remained remarkably constant, and continues to be the principal goal of both U.S. foreign policy and U.S. military strategy. No less remarkably constant has been the combination of military means upon which the United States has relied to fulfill the goal of containment; nuclear deterrence, deployment of conventional forces in threatened areas overseas, and a system of military alliances designed to supplement U.S. military power.

The purpose of the following chapters is to trace the evolution of declared U.S. military strategy since 1945 in the context of available military resources dedicated to its fulfillment. Particular emphasis is accorded the relationship between U.S. military obligations overseas and conventional force levels. As will be seen, since World War II there has never been a reasonable harmony of U.S. military aspirations and resources, although both have recorded significant changes over the years.

As has been noted, however, a disparity between commitments and force levels is not dangerous in and of itself. Commitments that are not threatened, or at least not threatened simultaneously, can be sustained by force levels smaller than those needed to defend all of them at the same time. The same may be said of commitments facing threats that can be effectively deterred by means other than conventional forces. Finally, commitments facing threats that are inherently difficult to generate quickly, thus allowing the defense to mobilize additional resources, can be effectively "covered" in peacetime by "inadequate" standing forces. It is thus important to keep in mind, in assessing the protection of vital U.S. security interests abroad, the distinctions between sequential and simultaneous threats; between deterrence and defense; between nuclear and non-nuclear forces as means of deterrence and defense; and between immediate threats "in place" and those requiring time to materialize.

CHAPTER 1.
CONTAINMENT VIA NUCLEAR SUPREMACY, 1945–1960

The policy of containment was first officially proclaimed by President Truman in 1947 in what became known as the Truman Doctrine. Speaking on behalf of economic and security assistance funds requested to assist Greece, facing a Soviet-sponsored internal insurgency, and Turkey, under severe pressure from Moscow to relinquish control of the Dardanelles, President Truman said:

I believe that it must be the policy of the United States to support free peoples who are resisting attempted subjugation by armed minorities or by outside pressures.

In support of this policy the Truman Administration sought to rebuild the war-torn economies of Europe through such spectacular ventures as the Marshall Plan. Until 1950 economic recovery was regarded as the most effective means of containing further Communist expansion on the Continent. Economic recovery, it was believed, would eliminate Europe's vulnerability to Communist-inspired revolutions and at the same time create the foundation for the rearmament necessary to thwart external aggression. To provide a military shield behind which economic recovery could proceed unimpeded, the Administration entered into a number of bilateral and collective security treaties with threatened nations. The scope of these commitments, which soon extended beyond the Western Hemisphere and the North Atlantic area, was staggering for a nation with a long history of avoiding foreign entanglements. In the space of just four years, from 1947 to 1951, the Administration entered into formal alliances with a total of 41 countries, including the Rio Treaty of 1947, the NATO Treaty of 1949, the ANZUS Treaty of 1951, and the Japanese and Philippine security treaties of 1951.

The principal military means available to implement those commitments was an effective monopoly of deliverable nuclear weapons. Although a declaratory U.S. military strategy based on the threat of instant nuclear retaliation against the homelands of aggressor states was not adopted until the advent of the Eisenhower Administration, primary reliance on nuclear weapons as a means of deterring aggression was the hallmark of U.S. strategy throughout the period 1945–1960.

During those years the United States enjoyed, first, a monopoly of nuclear weapons, and, subsequently, a decisive superiority. U.S. conventional force planning, heavily influenced by severe budgetary constraints (except during the

Korean War), reflected an assumption that nuclear weapons could provide a cheap and effective substitute for large ground, naval, and tactical air forces. Despite the proliferation of U.S. defense commitments overseas, U.S. conventional force levels remained far below those needed to fulfill those commitments in the event that nuclear deterrence failed. Nor, in the event of major conflict, could the United States expect much help from its European allies, who emerged from World War II economically and militarily prostrate. The sole exception was Great Britain, which retained a sizable conscripted army and a navy second only to that of the United States. Forces potentially available from France's impressive military recovery in the 1950s were otherwise engaged in defense of a crumbling colonial empire; during the period 1953–1955 French deployments to Indochina and North Africa reduced standing M-Day NATO ground forces in Europe by approximately one-third.

Confidence in the deterrent power of America's atomic arsenal was attended by profound public and congressional reluctance to invite involvement in a third major ground war on the Eurasian landmass. It is doubtful whether the United States would have ratified the NATO Treaty in 1949 had not the Truman Administration repeatedly reassured the Senate that U.S. membership entailed no obligation to deploy American ground forces on the Continent over and above the weak occupation forces already there. When the Administration, two years later, in the wake of the outbreak of the Korean War, proposed sending additional U.S. ground troops to Europe, a sense-of-the-Senate resolution was passed urging prior congressional approval. A major, permanent U.S. ground combat force presence in Europe was neither desired nor foreseen in the late 1940s and early 1950s.

Equally notable were the twin assumptions implicit in contemporary U.S. and allied operational plans for Europe's defense: (1) that a successful ground defense of Central Europe was at best problematical, given the disparity in opposing forces (an early U.S. plan, OFFTACKLE, envisaged a final defensive line in the Pyrenees); and, therefore, (2) that a Soviet invasion could ultimately be defeated only indirectly, through a sustained atomic bombing campaign against the U.S.S.R.'s industrial base and logistical infrastructure. Underlying all plans was a distinct and in some cases (e.g., the Western European Union defense plan of 1948–1949) formal division of military labor, with the Europeans supplying the bulk of the ground and supporting air forces and the United States providing the lion's share of nuclear, naval, and long-range air forces. This division of labor was no less implicit in the Eisenhower Administration's strategy of massive retaliation.

Not even the fall of China in 1949 and the outbreak of the Korean War in 1950, conflicts that raised serious questions about the utility of nuclear supremacy as a means of deterring limited or indirect communist aggression outside Europe, induced any lasting expansion in U.S. general purpose force levels. Those events did spark plans for U.S. and NATO conventional force increases, but those plans were never implemented. The postwar U.S. strategic focus remained riveted on a general war, defined as a massive Soviet attack on Europe that could be deterred or ultimately defeated by the threatened or actual invocation of the U.S. nuclear deterrent; indeed, many American policymakers initially regarded the invasion of South Korea as a diversionary prelude to a Soviet push into Europe.

Deliberate reliance on the deterrent value of U.S. nuclear supremacy stemmed from two factors. The first was a genuine conviction that nuclear weapons rendered large conventional forces more or less unnecessary. As noted by the late American military historian Russell F. Weigley,

> . . . to most Americans, including most of the government, the Army in the late 1940s seemed almost irrelevant to the Communist challenge. So pervasive was this attitude that the Army itself appears to have suffered increasingly under a sense of its own irrelevance, with consequent damage to energy and efficiency. To the extent that Americans saw the Communist threat as a military threat, their answer to it was simply the American atomic monopoly. If the Communists should—incredibly— resort to overt military force, the sequel, Americans assumed, must be full-scale war; and the United States would win such a war with air-atomic power.[1]

Neither overt Communist aggression in Asia nor Soviet acquisition of nuclear weapons altered the U.S. commitment to what in 1954 became codified as the strategy of massive nuclear retaliation. The prevailing view remained that nuclear weapons offered an inexpensive and effective substitute for conventional forces, especially ground forces. Even so-called "tactical" or "battlefield" nuclear weapons were regarded as effective trade-offs against traditional ground combat formations. Thus reasoned General Alfred M. Gruenther, Supreme Allied Commander Europe, in 1954: "If seventy divisions . . . are needed to establish a conventional line of defense between the Alps and the Baltic, then seventy minus X divisions equipped with atomic weapons would be needed."[2]

Of the three armed services it was not surprising that the Air Force, and particularly its Strategic Air Command (SAC), emerged as the most vocal champion of massive retaliation. Until the late 1950s, SAC possessed a virtual monopoly of the means of delivering nuclear weapons against the Soviet Union, and many Air Force leaders believed that the combination of the long-range bomber (the B-29, followed by the B-36, B-47, and B-52) and the H-bomb had at last made possible the realization of the "victory-through-airpower" theories of Douhet, Mitchell, and Seversky. During the latter 1950s, the Air Force received over 45 percent of the defense budget; U.S. ground forces and other general purpose forces, including tactical air components, were starved in order to feed the Strategic Air Command.

To be sure, not everyone regarded nuclear weapons as a panacea for the abyss separating U.S. postwar military obligations abroad and non-nuclear force capabilities. During the 1950s there arose a school of thought, centered largely in the Army and the defense intellectual community, that rejected the premises of massive retaliation and pressed for conventional force renewal. Advocates of what later became known as "flexible response," however, failed to exert any profound influence on declared U.S. military strategy until the Kennedy Administration.

The second factor encouraging reliance on nuclear supremacy was money— or, to put it more accurately, the perceived lack of it. At no time during the period 1945–1960 was the public, the Congress, or the Executive Branch prepared to make the fiscal and economic sacrifices necessary to provide a level of general purpose forces commensurate with burgeoning U.S. defense commitments in Europe and East Asia. Both the Truman and Eisenhower Administrations imposed stringent limits on military spending in peacetime that compelled disproportionate reliance on nuclear weapons and strategic airpower at the expense of investment in relatively costly ground, naval, and tactical air forces. Confronted in 1945– 1946 with irresistible public pressure for rapid demobilization of U.S. forces from their wartime levels and for a swift conversion of the economy from war to peace, the Truman Administration was in no position to match its new overseas commitments with appropriate conventional force levels.

The fiscally conservative Eisenhower Administration was convinced that America's first line of defense was a sound, vibrant economy. President Eisenhower himself believed that large military expenditures would destroy the very free market economy the military was charged with defending. He was, moreover, persuaded that the combination of nuclear supremacy, overseas alliance systems, and covert action could in large measure offset the need for massive U.S. conventional forces. Although defense spending as a percentage of the gross national product averaged over 10 percent during the Eisenhower years (see Appendix B), defense dollars continued to be allocated disproportionately to meet the requirements of massive retaliation. As then-Air Force Chief of Staff Nathan Twining testified before the Senate Armed Services Committee in the early 1950s, "a new strategy built around the use of atomic weapons" was necessary to permit the United States "to reduce our forces considerably" and the "only way we can provide the forces for the country within a reasonable standard of financing."[3]

The impact upon U.S. general purpose force levels of the push for rapid postwar demobilization, fiscal austerity, and faith in the deterrent value of nuclear supremacy was evident throughout the period in the changes registered in the authorized active-duty personnel end-strengths of the three services; in the number of Army divisions; and in the number of U.S. Navy combatant ships (see Appendices C, D, and E).

It is worth noting that the strategy of massive retaliation, which called for the invocation of nuclear weapons at times and places of U.S. choosing, sought to apply U.S. strength against Soviet weakness. The Eisenhower Administration rejected the proposition underlying what later became known as flexible response—that the United States should develop military forces capable of effectively responding to aggression at any level and wherever it might occur. President Eisenhower regarded America's nuclear arsenal and its naval and tactical air supremacy as natural military advantages to be employed against Soviet military weaknesses; he was highly skeptical of the U.S. ability to prevail in a major land war against Communist forces on the Eurasian landmass, which would entail pitting American weakness against Communist strength on grounds chosen by Moscow, Peking, or their satellites. It was this skepticism that in large part prompted Eisenhower's refusal to commit U.S. combat forces on behalf of France's struggle to retain Indochina. Yet, if the collapse of French arms there in 1954 proved anything, it proved the superfluity of massive retaliation as a deterrent to non-Soviet Communist aggression outside Europe.

> Never was the difference between the verbal intransigence and the practical prudence of the new Republican team in Washington more disastrously demonstrated than during these feverish weeks [of the Dienbienphu crisis], when threats in Washington of a preventive war against China alternated with assurances to the electorate that the United States would in no circumstances engage in "another Korean war." Never did the so-called strategy of "massive reprisals," that lame compromise between the crusading spirit and the spirit of budgetary economy, more strikingly demonstrate its incapacity to respond to the limited reversals, the local conflicts and the pin-pricks which constitute the daily fare of international politics. Reduced to the sole device of threatening apocalyptic war on every occasion, it sowed terror among America's allies and proteges without making much impression on her enemies, and finally ended in resounding inaction.[4]

Despite the inevitable failure of a strategy designed to contain non-nuclear Communist aggression in "peripheral" areas through the threat of nuclear retaliation, President Eisenhower nevertheless correctly perceived an inherent division of military labor between the United States and its overseas allies, with the latter providing most of the ground forces necessary to contain Communist expansion and the United States supplying the nuclear, naval, and air components of the collective defense. As President Eisenhower himself put it, in language that foreshadowed that of the Nixon Doctrine of the following decade, a major function of the U.S. system of overseas alliances was "to develop within the various areas and regions of the free world indigenous forces for the maintenance of order, the safeguarding of frontiers, and the provision of the bulk of ground capability." When asked whether this meant that U.S. allies should bear the brunt of fighting a future war, Eisenhower replied that "that was the kernel of the whole thing."[5] Eisenhower envisaged the role of U.S. ground forces as that of a central mobile reserve for the Free World, a reflection of his own aversion to their use in foreign conflicts. Although forward deployment of some U.S. ground forces in Europe and elsewhere overseas was necessary to underline American treaty commitments, Eisenhower believed that the primary burden of local defense ought to rest on the combination of indigenous local ground forces and U.S. sea and air power; the bulk of the U.S. Army would be withheld "on tap" in the United States as potential reinforcements for local defenses that proved unable to hold the line. As U.S. defense commitments overseas expanded, however, so too did the proportion of the U.S. Army deployed there, a development that made it increasingly difficult to maintain a robust and ready central reserve in the United States. Token forward deployments became major and more or less permanent garrisons, with first claim on the best units and equipment. The tug-of-war between forward deployment and the concept of a central reserve continues to this day, the latest manifestation of the latter being the Rapid Deployment Force.

Even when considered in conjunction with allied military resources and the concept of the U.S. Army as a central reserve, there remained throughout the period 1945–1960 a significant gap between U.S. conventional force levels and commitments. This mismatch between strategy and forces did not go unnoticed, especially by those who had serious reservations about the utility of massive nuclear responses, threatened or actual, to certain kinds of aggression. In the early 1950s, spurred by Communist aggression in Asia and by Soviet acquisition of nuclear weapons much sooner than anticipated, two major attempts were made to bring force levels into some reasonable balance with defense commitments. Although both attempts failed, they revealed the degree of divergence between U.S. military obligations and capabilities that characterized the period.

NSC-68

The first attempt began shortly before the outbreak of the Korean War and was reflected in a National Security Council Memorandum known as NSC-68, which was prepared by a small ad hoc group of State and Defense Department representatives under the direction of the Chairman of the State Department's Policy Planning Staff, Paul Nitze. Soviet acquisition of the atomic bomb in 1949 and the triumph of Communism in China in the same year encouraged a more militant approach to containment and demonstrated the need for expanded investment in general purpose forces for conflicts in which the threat or use of nuclear weapons was inappropriate. The subsequent outbreak of the Korean War validated the indispensability of larger non-nuclear force levels; during that conflict the U.S. Army ultimately mobilized some 2,834,000 men and 20 divisions, eight of which (along with one Marine Corps division) were deployed to Korea.

A central premise of NSC-68 was that the Soviet Union at some point during the 1950s would develop credible nuclear retaliatory capabilities, thereby undercutting the value of the U.S. nuclear arsenal as a deterrent even to overt Soviet aggression.

NSC-68 called for what in effect was a militarization of what had until 1950 been a policy of containing Communist expansion primarily through economic and security assistance to threatened states. The document accorded primary emphasis to the defense of Europe, an emphasis that prevailed within the Administration even after the outbreak of the Korean War, and one that continues to this day. That conflict was initially viewed by many as an attempt by Moscow to divert U.S. military resources away from Europe. It was during the Korean War that the decision was made to deploy from four to six U.S. Army divisions in Europe on an indefinite basis, a decision that the U.S. military supported only on condition that West Germany be rearmed and its forces incorporated into the NATO defense structure.

NSC-68 did not propose a specific level of conventional forces, leaving that task instead to the Joint Chiefs of Staff. The Joint Chiefs of Staff, after rejecting an initial assessment that would have exceeded any conceivable defense budget, finally recommended a force of 27 Army and Marine Corps divisions, 408 warships, and 41 Air Force and Marine Corps fighter-attack wings. Those force levels were never funded. The combination of postwar demobilization, the "fiscal policies of the Eisenhower administration and the mystique of nuclear weapons had virtually eradicated the concept of flexible response—at least temporarily."[6]

Following the end of the Korean War, U.S. general purpose forces were allowed quickly to atrophy to a level substantially below those believed necessary by the Joint Chiefs of Staff on the basis of NSC-68. As shown in Table 1, by 1959 the impact of primary reliance on a strategy of massive nuclear retaliation on the gap between conventional force levels and requirements had become profound. The gap was not merely one of size but also one of quality, since not all of the 24 Air Force and Marine Corps fighter-attack wings and only 11 of the Army's 14 divisions were regarded as combat-ready. Conventional force readiness as well as personnel end-strengths were sacrificed on the altar of massive retaliation.

The one notable exception to this general trend was a dramatic expansion in U.S. forces deployed in the European theater, which grew from 145,000 personnel in 1950 to 427,000 by the end of 1953, an almost threefold increase (see Appendix F).

TABLE 1. U.S. General Purpose
Force Levels and Requirements During the 1950s

TYPE OF FORCE	NSC-68/JCS REQUIREMENTS	FORCES ON HAND 1959	SHORTFALL
Army/USMC divisions	27	17	10 (37%)
Major U.S. Navy surface combatants	408	376	32 (19%)
Air Force/USMC fighter-attack wings	41	24	17 (42%)

Source: Based on information provided in William W. Kaufmann, *Planning Conventional Forces 1950–1980* (Washington, D.C.: The Brookings Institution, 1982).

THE LISBON GOALS

Like NSC-68 and its attendant JCS recommendations, the second attempt at conventional force renewal was stimulated primarily by the loss of America's nuclear monopoly and by continued Communist expansion in Asia. Meeting in Lisbon in early 1952, representatives of the member states of the North Atlantic Treaty Organization endorsed recommendations for expanded general purpose forces, including ground combat forces totalling 96 active and quickly mobilizable reserve divisions, 75 of which were to be deployed in defense of NATO's Central Front. Such a force was believed to be the minimum necessary to defend NATO Europe against a Soviet army estimated to contain 140–175 divisions, 25 of which were deployed forward in Central Europe. At the time of the Lisbon meeting only a dozen or so scattered, understrength U.S. and allied divisions were deployed in Europe.

The Libson conventional force goals proved to be as politically and economically unattainable as those of the Joint Chiefs of Staff following NSC-68. The incoming Eisenhower Administration's doctrine of massive retaliation explicitly abjured attempts to counterbalance local Soviet conventional force preponderance in Europe or elsewhere by means other than nuclear weapons. Moreover, neither the fiscally conservative Eisenhower Administration nor U.S. allies, still heavily immersed in postwar reconstruction of their devastated economies, were prepared to finance their respective shares of the 96-division force. Additionally,

> . . . the NATO Treaty was not conceived—at least by many of its architects—as a vehicle for actually redressing NATO's military inferiority. Rather, its purpose was to clarify American intentions regarding any Soviet attempt to change further the European balance of power. Such a visible United States commitment to Europe . . . backed by U.S. nuclear might would be sufficient to stop Soviet expansion.[7]

The end result was a comparatively modest expansion in NATO conventional force levels, attributable in large part to the re-creation of a German Army following that country's admission to NATO in 1955. In 1957 the Lisbon force goals were formally reduced from 96 active and ready reserve divisions to a 30-division standing force dedicated to the defense of the Central Front and lacking any significant reserve back-up. It was widely believed—or hoped—that deployment of U.S. tactical nuclear weapons in Europe, which began in 1953, would offset continued Soviet preponderance in conventional forces along the inter-German border.

It is perhaps testimony to the persistence of conventional force shortfalls within NATO that even today the Alliance deploys but 26 active full-strength division in the Central Front Region.[8]

NOTES

1. Russell F. Weigley, *History of the United States Army* (New York: Macmillan Publishing Co., Inc., 1967), p. 501.

2. Alfred M. Gruenther, quoted in Robert Endicott Osgood, *NATO: The Entangling Alliance* (Chicago: University of Chicago Press, 1962), p. 109.
3. Ibid. p. 122.
4. Herbert Leuthy, *France Against Herself* (New York: Praeger, 1955), p. 459.
5. Dwight D. Eisenhower, quoted in John Lewis Gaddis, *Strategies of Containment, A Critical Appraisal of Postwar American National Security Policy* (New York: Oxford University Press, 1982), p. 153.
6. William W. Kaufmann, *Planning Conventional Forces 1950–1980* (Washington, D.C.: The Brookings Institution, 1982), p. 3.
7. Alain C. Enthoven and K. Wayne Smith, *How Much Is Enough? Shaping the Defense Program, 1961–1969* (New York: Harper & Row, 1971), p. 118.
8. Anthony H. Cordesman, "The NATO Central Region and the Balance of Uncertainty," *Armed Forces Journal* (July, 1983), p. 23.

CHAPTER 2.
FLEXIBLE RESPONSE
AND THE 2½-WAR STRATEGY, 1961–1968

The military strategy of the Kennedy Administration explicitly rejected the premises of massive retaliation. Heavily swayed by the theories of such longstanding critics of massive retaliation as Maxwell D. Taylor, William W. Kaufmann, Robert E. Osgood, Henry Kissinger, and B. H. Liddel Hart, the

> . . . leaders of the Kennedy Administration faced up to the fact that nuclear weapons, whether strategic or tactical, could not be a substitute for adequate conventional forces. They also recognized that existing conventional forces were inadequate to meet worldwide commitments without the use of nuclear weapons.[1]

As Taylor put it in 1959 in his influential book, *The Uncertain Trumpet*,

> It is my belief that Massive Retaliation as a guiding strategic concept has reached a dead end and that there is an urgent need for a reappraisal of our strategic needs. In its heyday, Massive Retaliation could offer our leaders only two choices, the initiation of general nuclear war or compromise and retreat. From its earliest days, many world events have occurred which cast doubt on its validity and exposed its fallacious character. Korea, a limited conventional war, fought by the United States when we had an atomic monopoly, was clear disproof of its universal efficacy. The many other limited wars which have occurred since 1945—the Chinese civil war, the guerrilla warfare in Greece and Malaya, Vietnam, Taiwan, Hungary, the Middle East, Laos, to mention only a few—are clear evidence that, while our massive retaliatory strategy may have prevented the Great War—a World War III—it has not maintained the Little Peace; that is, peace from disturbances which are little only in comparison with the disaster of general war.
>
> The strategic doctrine which I would propose to replace Massive Retaliation is called herein the Strategy of Flexible Response. This name suggests the need for a capability to react across the entire spectrum of possible challenge, for coping with anything from general atomic war to infiltrations and aggressions such as threaten Laos and Berlin in 1959. The new strategy would recognize that it is just as necessary to deter or win quickly a limited war as to deter general war. Otherwise, the limited war which we cannot win quickly may result in our piecemeal attrition or involvement in an expanding conflict which may grow into the general war we all want to avoid.[2]

Nor did the Kennedy Administration share its predecessor's fiscal conservatism and conviction that large defense budgets endangered America's social and economic well-being. Indeed, as late as 1968, at the height of the Vietnam War, Secretary of Defense Robert S. McNamara was still persuaded that

> . . . embracing the obligations of international leadership need not force us to divert badly needed resources from the improvement of American domestic society. Our resources are sufficient, if wisely allocated and if we have the will, to meet the needs of the weak and underprivileged both at home and abroad. For the sake of our security and our well-being, we can afford no less.[3]

Accordingly, a major expansion in U.S. general purpose forces was launched, an expansion that peaked during the Vietnam War. During the period 1961–1964, the size of the U.S. Army was increased from 859,000 men and 14 divisions to 927,000 men and 16 divisions, and that of the Navy from 627,000 men and 624 combatant ships to 668,000 men and 754 combatant ships (see Appendices C and D). Although the number of Air Force fighter-attack aircraft declined largely because of the impact of modernization on unit cost, Air Force active-duty personnel end-strength rose from 821,000 to 857,000. Major improvements in the capabilities and readiness of U.S. conventional forces also were undertaken.

The essence of the Kennedy Administration's strategy of flexible response, proclaimed in 1962 and formally adopted by NATO five years later, was to create conventional forces adequate to meet non-nuclear Communist aggression without an immediate resort to nuclear weapons, while at the same time maintaining a level of nuclear superiority that would permit the United States, in the event that conventional defenses proved inadequate, to dominate escalation of any conflict. The basic premise underlying flexible response, which remains NATO's declared strategy, is that the advent of secure Soviet nuclear retaliatory capabilities at both the intercontinental and theater levels, by lessening the credibility of nuclear responses to non-nuclear attack, makes essential the establishment of a conventional force posture capable of deterring and defeating such attacks without at least early reliance on nuclear forces. Flexible response thus confines the use of nuclear weapons to circumstances in which the enemy employs them first, or the defeat of U.S. and allied conventional forces appears imminent and irreversible.

During the 1960s conventional force expansion was accompanied by major quantitative and qualitative increases in U.S. intercontinental and theater nuclear forces. The defense of Europe, moreover, remained the primary focus of U.S. force planners, despite the increasing diversion of U.S. military resources to Southeast Asia in the latter half of the decade. The effect of Vietnam (and the defusing of the 1961 Berlin crisis) on U.S. force levels in Europe was evident in their decline from 416,000 personnel in 1962 to 300,000 in 1969 (see Appendix F). Paradoxically, the United States maintained larger general purpose force levels in Europe during the era of massive retaliation—a strategy calling for "trip-wire" conventional forces—than it has since the inception of flexible response. During the period 1953–1960 annual end-strength of U.S. personnel deployed in the U.S. European Command geographical area averaged 395,750, compared to an annual average of 333,400 from 1961 to 1982.

Conventional force requirements during both the Kennedy and Johnson Administrations were calculated against the backdrop of a plethora of overseas military commitments undertaken by the Truman and Eisenhower Administrations. By early 1961 the United States was committed by treaty to defend 45 countries in Europe, the Far East, and the Western hemisphere, and had informally extended security guarantees to a number of others. About half of the countries that the United States was committed to defend were on or near the borders of the Soviet Union and China, both of which, in conjunction with their respective military partners, were regarded as implacable foes pursuing highly coordinated expansionist foreign and defense policies vis-à-vis the United States and its allies.

Until the late 1960s U.S. foreign policy and military planning rested on the assumption that China was little more than an obedient servant of Soviet imperialism. President Kennedy himself defined the entire Communist world as "a monolithic and ruthless conspiracy,"[4] a view that was fully shared by his vice president and successor in the White House. The Communist threat was regarded as virtually unlimited in scope, ranging from a potential nuclear attack on the United States to the subversion of pro-Western regimes throughout the Third World via "wars of national liberation." The Kennedy and Johnson Administrations' obsession with the latter was reflected in attempts to create effective counterinsurgency forces and, ultimately, in America's increasing entanglement in Vietnam. Unlike the selective brand of containment pursued by the Eisenhower Administration, Presidents Kennedy and Johnson applied containment indiscriminately, even when it involved—as was the case in Vietnam—pitting U.S. weakness against Communist advantage.

The combination of extensive overseas defense commitments and the postulation of a monolithic and unlimited Communist threat raised the prospect of being confronted by multiple, simultaneous aggression in two or more theaters of operation. It was this prospect that led the Kennedy Administration to adopt the so-called 2½-war concept as the basis for U.S. conventional force planning. The concept called for forces sufficient to deal simultaneously with a Warsaw Pact invasion of Europe, a Chinese attack in Asia, and a "lesser" contingency elsewhere or not directly involving Soviet or Chinese forces.

According to William W. Kaufmann, the forces required to meet the demands of the 2½-war concept were estimated by the Pentagon in 1962 to encompass a total of 28.33 Army and Marine Corps divisions and 41 Air Force and Marine Corps fighter-attack wings,[5] a force level almost identical to that proposed by the Joint Chiefs of Staff in response to NSC-68. Underlying this calculation were numerous postulations regarding anticipated allied contributions, the likely nature and duration of specific contingencies, and the role of reserve and National Guard forces, which were expected to account for over one-third of the 28.33 division–41 fighter-attack wing requirement.

Central to the 2½-war concept was the withholding of major forces in the United States as a strategic reserve, which under the Kennedy Administration was embodied in the U.S. Strike Command, created in 1962 and consisting mainly of designated U.S. Army units. Creation of a large pool of active and reserve ground and tactical air forces at home was deemed essential to offset the inherent inflexibility and greater costs associated with U.S. forces deployed overseas. A large strategic reserve was believed to be no less essential as a hedge against unexpected contingencies and as a rotation base for a prolonged war.

It became increasingly evident that stationing U.S. forces in threatened areas such as Western Europe and Korea not only made them less available for service elsewhere, but it also imposed heavy economic and political costs on the United States. The more units that could be brought back to the United States, the greater their potential availability for worldwide use and the lower the total cost. Instead of having conventional forces dedicated to every theater of any consequence . . . with staggering implications for force size and cost, a strategic reserve could be established at home. From that favorable geographic position, specially tailored expeditionary forces could be dispatched quickly to trouble spots wherever they might be, if they could be given the necessary long-range mobility. Fortunately, the advent of intercontinental, high-speed, large-payload, wide-bodied jet aircraft seemed to solve the problem. Combined with a minimum of overseas deployments, some prepositioning of materiel in sensitive theaters such as Western Europe, and fast-deployment logistics ships that would serve as floating and mobile depots for heavy equipment and supplies, a large fleet of cargo jets would ensure that intercontinental mobility could substitute for forces frozen in all theaters of primary interest to the United States.[6]

In the absence of a sufficient strategic reserve, serving in effect as a force multiplier, it was estimated that 55 divisions and 82 fighter-attack wings would be necessary to meet the forward-deployment requirements "in all theaters of primary interest to the United States."[7]

The effectiveness of the strategic reserve, however, was contingent upon the ability to move the Strike Command's forces and other units suitable for rapid deployment overseas in a timely fashion, and to protect the lines of communication between the United States and units so deployed. The strategic reserve had to have at its disposal sufficient strategic mobility in the form of large transport aircraft, specialized shipping, and, where appropriate, sets of equipment prepositioned in likely areas of need. On the basis of estimated strategic mobility requirements, Secretary of Defense Robert S. McNamara requested from Congress authorization to procure 120 C-5A and 284 C-141 aircraft, 31 fast deployment logistics ships, and three division sets of equipment slated for prepositioning in Europe.

An effective strategic reserve also demanded substantial naval forces capable of quickly gaining and maintaining control of the vast expanses of water separating the continental United States from potential trouble spots on or along the Eurasian landmass. This requirement, together with those related to other naval missions and to the perceived political necessity to maintain two carrier task forces (subsequently relabelled carrier battlegroups) in the Mediterranean and two in the Western Pacific at all times, produced an estimated force requirement of 607 ships (excluding SSBNs), including 15 carriers, 266 surface warships, and 102 amphibious assault vessels. As will be seen, these force requirements, like those postulated for strategic mobility, were never fulfilled during the 1960s, leaving much of the strategic reserve in the event of major conflict in the position of a person stranded at home on New Year's Eve for want of a taxi.

The tables appearing in Appendices C, D, and E show the changes registered in selected U.S. conventional force levels during the period 1961–1968. It is apparent that the substitution of flexible response for massive retaliation had a significant impact on the size of U.S. ground and tactical air forces well before 1965, when U.S. general purpose force levels were expanded further to meet the mounting demands of the Vietnam War.

Whether they were sufficient to fight 2½ wars simultaneously, however, is highly doubtful. The ½-war in Vietnam consumed far more than a ½-war's worth of U.S. conventional forces. Of the 8,744,000 Americans who were on active duty from August 1964 to January 1973, a total of 3,403,000 served in Southeast Asia. In 1968, at the height of U.S. involvement in that conflict, some 550,000 U.S. troops were deployed in Southeast Asia out of a total active-duty U.S. military end-strength of 3,547,000. Of the Army's 19 divisions, seven were deployed in Vietnam along with elements of three more. Also deployed in the region were two of the Marine Corps' three divisions and nine of the Air Force's 28 tactical fighter wings. These forward-deployed forces, together with their much larger rotation base in the United States, represented the bulk of U.S. conventional forces on hand.

Had the Soviets invaded Europe in 1968 (as some feared after their invasion of Czechoslovakia), the United States would have been in no position to provide sufficient conventional forces to deal with such a 1½-war scenario, to say nothing of dealing with, for example, a simultaneous Chinese invasion of South Korea (as noted, the Korean conflict of 1950–1953 engaged a total of nine Army and Marine Corps divisions, seven more than the number deployed in Korea in the late 1960s). This suggests that the force goals of 28 divisions and 41 tactical fighter-attack wings, even though they were eventually achieved, were woefully inadequate to fulfill the requirements of declared U.S. military strategy. As Henry Kissinger has concluded, "We never chose to build the conventional forces envisaged by the ambitious strategy. In military terms the two-and-one-half war strategy was a paper exercise. . . . "[8]

This mismatch between strategy and forces was further compounded by the failure to provide the strategic mobility necessary to ensure timely and unimpeded responsiveness of forces assigned to the strategic reserve. Although a large strategic reserve was created, in part through withdrawal of selected units from overseas, programs designed to secure their swift and safe redeployment in the event of a crisis or war were never fully funded by the Congress. As shown in Table 2, although the goal of 28.33 divisions and 41 tactical fighter-attack wings was eventually more or less fulfilled, the Congress refused to fund a 607-ship navy or the 404 C-5A and C-141 aircraft and 31 fast-deployment logistics ships requested by Secretary of Defense McNamara. Especially hard hit were requests

TABLE 2. Conventional Forces Planned
During the 1960s and Existing in 1981

FORCE COMPONENT	PLANNED	EXISTING
Divisions		
Active Army	16	16
Active Marine Corps	3	3
Reserve Army	8	8
Reserve Marine Corps	1	1
Total	28	28
Fighter-attack wings		
Active Air Force	26	26
Active Marine Corps	3	3
Reserve Air Force	11	11
Reserve Marine Corps	1	1
Total	41	41
General purpose naval forces		
Attack carriers	15	12
Surface warships	266	188
Nuclear-powered attack submarines	90	82
Underway replenishment ships	60	56
Amphibious assault ships	102	59
Mine countermeasure ships	18	3
Auxiliary ships	56	40
Total	607	440
Strategic mobility capabilities		
Prepositioned sets of division equipment	3	4
C-5A aircraft	120	70
C-141 aircraft	284	234
Fast deployment logistics ships	31	7

Source: Adapted from a table appearing in William W. Kaufmann, *U.S. Conventional Force Planning 1950–1980* (Washington, D.C.: The Brookings Institution, 1982), p. 14.

for C-5As, fast-deployment logistics ships, and amphibious assault ships, which in the view of many members of the Congress represented the kind of capabilities whose very possession invited further American military "adventures" abroad like the increasingly unpopular war in Vietnam.

In sum, although the decision of the Kennedy Administration to discard the strategy of massive retaliation in favor of flexible response was clearly justified in light of the declining credibility of nuclear responses to non-nuclear aggression, neither the Kennedy nor Johnson Administrations succeeded in creating sufficient conventional forces to fight 2½ wars simultaneously, judged to be the proper basis for conventional force planning.

To be sure, goals for expanded ground and tactical air forces were set and eventually fulfilled. Those goals, however, were themselves inadequate, certainly if measured against the drain on U.S. conventional military resources caused by the ½-war in Vietnam. They were, moreover, predicated on the availability of a large, highly mobile strategic reserve, which proved politically impossible to create.

Indeed, to the extent that Vietnam represented a test of the strategy of flexible response, the strategy flunked. As John Lewis Gaddis has concluded:

> The American defeat there rather grew out of assumptions derived quite logically from that strategy: that the defense of Southeast Asia was crucial to the maintenance of world order; that force could be applied in Vietnam with precision and discrimination; that means existed accurately to evaluate performance; and that the effects would be to enhance American power, prestige, and credibility in the world. These assumptions in turn reflected a curiously myopic preoccupation with process — a disproportionate fascination with means at the expense of ends — with the result that a strategy designed to produce a precise correspondence between intentions and accomplishments in fact produced just the opposite.[9]

NOTES

1. Enthoven and Smith, *How Much is Enough?*, pp. 210–211.
2. Maxwell D. Taylor, *The Uncertain Trumpet* (New York: Harper Brothers, 1959), pp. 5–7.
3. Robert S. McNamara, *The Essence of Security* (New York: Harper & Row, 1968), p. 11.
4. John F. Kennedy, quoted in Gaddis, *Strategies of Containment* p. 208.
5. Kaufmann, *Planning Conventional Forces*, pp. 5–8.
6. Ibid. p. 8.
7. Ibid. p. 6.
8. Henry Kissinger, *The White House Years* (Boston: Little, Brown and Company, 1979), p. 220.
9. Ibid. p. 238.

CHAPTER 3.
VIETNAM, THE NIXON DOCTRINE, AND THE 1½-WAR STRATEGY, 1969–1979

The period 1969–1979 witnessed a significant contraction in the declared goals of U.S. military strategy and in levels of U.S. general purpose forces. Despite reductions in both, there persisted, as in preceding periods, a significant disparity between U.S. military power and obligations.

Largely in response to the disastrous American experience in Vietnam and to the collapse of any semblance of unity between China and the Soviet Union, the Nixon Administration undertook a major reduction in American military purpose and power in Asia. This reduction continued throughout the Ford Administration, despite an unparalleled expansion in Soviet military power that undermined the credibility of the U.S. nuclear deterrent and NATO's non-nuclear defenses.

U.S. retrenchment in Asia was heralded in 1969 by proclamation of the Nixon Doctrine and the elimination of the 2½-war concept as the basis for conventional force planning. The Nixon Doctrine, first enunciated by the President in Guam in July, 1969, represented a direct response to the unpopularity of the Vietnam War, and a determination to avoid U.S. involvement in another such conflict. Speaking to a group of reporters on the island, President Nixon stated:

> I believe the time has come when the United States, in our relations with all of our Asian friends, [should] be quite emphatic on two points: one, that we will keep our treaty commitments, for example with Thailand under SEATO; but, two, that as far as the problems of internal security are concerned, as far as the problems of military defense, except for the threat of a major power involving nuclear weapons, that the United States is going to encourage and has a right to expect that this problem will be increasingly handled by, and the responsibility for it taken by, the Asian nations themselves.[1]

The doctrine was further elaborated in President Nixon's first formal foreign policy report, on February 18, 1970:

> —The United States will keep all of its treaty commitments.

> —We shall provide a shield if a nuclear power threatens the freedom of a nation allied with us, or of a nation whose survival we consider vital to our security and the security of the region as a whole.

—In cases involving other types of aggression we shall furnish military and economic assistance when requested and as appropriate. But we shall look to the nation directly threatened to assume the primary responsibility of providing the manpower for its own defense.[2]

The Nixon Doctrine was a more limited and discriminating application of U.S. military containment of Communist expansion in Asia, with a determination to avoid American involvement in another Vietnam. The doctrine sought to encourage, via enhanced levels of U.S. security and economic assistance, American allies and client states in Asia to assume the "primary responsibility of providing the manpower" for their own defense. Subsequent interpretive statements by Administration officials made it plain that direct U.S. military intervention would if possible be restricted to employment of air and naval power and such other support as the beleaguered nations could not provide on their own. Manpower required for the ground battle, which such nations could supply, would be the main contribution of local allies resisting outside aggression. Like the Eisenhower Administration's approach to military containment, the Nixon Doctrine sought to apply U.S. strengths against Communist weaknesses while assigning to allies primary responsibility for the land battle.

Implicit in the Nixon Doctrine was a reduction in U.S. ground combat forces deployed forward in East Asia, and a sizable if not commensurate cut in Army personnel end-strength, and in fact this is what happened. Beginning in 1969 phased withdrawals of U.S. ground forces from Vietnam were undertaken in tandem with President Nixon's policy of Vietnamization, which called for progressive South Vietnamese assumption of responsibility for the land battle, aided by increased U.S. security assistance. At about the same time, one of the Army's two divisions stationed in Korea was withdrawn to the United States, and selected ground and tactical air units were removed from Japan and Thailand. The U.S. impulse to retrench in Asia continued for eight years, culminating in President Carter's proposal, successfully resisted by the Congress, to withdraw the Army's one remaining division in Korea.

The impact of U.S. retrenchment in Asia was evident in the disparity between pre-Vietnam (1964) U.S. conventional force levels and those of the latter 1970s. In 1964, U.S. active-duty military personnel end-strength totalled 2,687,000; by 1979 it had dwindled to but 2,024,000, a decrease of almost 25 percent. During the same period U.S. Air Force end-strength shrank from 857,000 to 559,000 personnel, and that of the Navy from 668,000 to 524,000. The Army declined from a pre-Vietnam strength of 973,000 men and 16 divisions to a force of 759,000 men and 13 divisions.

To be sure, the Nixon Doctrine's redefinition of U.S. military containment of communist aggression in Asia was but one of several factors behind the contraction of U.S. conventional force levels in the 1970s. In the wake of Vietnam there was little support for the kind of defense budgets that would have been necessary to maintain even pre-Vietnam force levels. The combination of public and Congressional resistance to rebuilding U.S. military power, and the Nixon, Ford, and Carter Administrations' pursuit of détente with the Soviet Union and normalization of relations with China, made life very difficult for those who, like Secretary of Defense James Schlesinger, advocated larger defense budgets to counter the ongoing Soviet military buildup that had begun while U.S. military resources were being depleted in Vietnam. During the years 1969–1975, Administration defense requests suffered annual cuts at the hands of Congress averaging $6 billion, while nondefense spending requests were increased by an average of $4.7 billion.[3] As Kissinger has recalled, "In the anti-military orgy spawned by Vietnam, to have challenged the overwhelming Congressional sentiment for 'domestic priorities' was . . . an exercise in futility. . . ."[4] Indeed, real U.S. defense expenditure during the 1970s declined to levels well below those of the last pre-Vietnam years. In fiscal 1964 the U.S. defense budget, measured in terms of outlays in constant 1983 dollars, amounted to $181.6 billion; by fiscal 1976 the budget had bottomed out to $155.1 billion (see Appendix A). This adverse trend was reversed only in the latter half of the decade, when the Carter Administration boosted the defense outlays from $157.9 billion in fiscal 1977 (in constant 1983 dollars) to $170 billion in fiscal 1980.

A no less important influence on U.S. conventional force levels during the period 1969–1979 was the Nixon Administration's abandonment of the 2½-war concept as the basis for general purpose force planning, replacing it with what was explicitly declared to be a "1½-war strategy." The principal reason given for this change was that by the late 1960s China and the Soviet Union were no longer allies, but enemies, making it highly improbable that the United States would be confronted by a simultaneous Warsaw Pact attack in Europe and a Chinese attack in Asia. As Henry Kissinger has noted in retrospect, "We had to give up the obsession with a Communist monolith. By linking Soviet and Chinese purposes we created presumptions that . . . ran counter to the demonstrable antagonism between the two major Communist powers."[5] On the contrary, China came to be viewed by many in the Nixon Administration as an invaluable strategic counterweight to the Soviet Union and even a possible wartime ally, and there is little question that strategic considerations were paramount in the administration's drive for normalized relations with Beijing.

A second reason given for moving to a 1½-war concept was the desire to bring U.S. military strategy into alignment with available military resources. The 1½-war concept

> . . . harmonized doctrine and capability. We had never generated the forces our two-and-one-half war doctrine required; the gap between our declaratory and our actual policy was bound to create confusion in the minds of potential aggressors and to raise grave risks if we attempted to apply it.[6]

Both the 1½-war concept and its rationales were succinctly laid out by President Nixon in 1970:

> In an effort to harmonize doctrine and capability, we chose what is best described as the "1½-war" strategy. Under it we will maintain in peacetime general purpose forces adequate for simultaneously meeting a major Communist attack in either Europe or Asia, assisting allies against non-Chinese threats in Asia, and contending with a contingency elsewhere.
>
> The choice of this strategy was based on the following considerations:
>
> —the nuclear capability of our strategic and theater nuclear forces serves as a deterrent to full-scale Soviet attack on NATO Europe or Chinese attack on our Asian allies;
>
> —the prospects for a coordinated two-front attack on our allies by Russia and China are low both because of the risks of nuclear war and the improbability of Sino-Soviet cooperation. . . .[7]

In effect, the 1½-war concept called for conventional forces sufficient to repel simultaneously a Warsaw Pact invasion of Western Europe and a "½-war" attack elsewhere. The most likely ½-war contingency, and the one most often used as the basis of conventional force planning, was a non-Chinese-sponsored North Korean invasion of South Korea. Western Europe and South Korea were then, as they are today, the only two places on the Eurasian landmass where substantial U.S. ground combat troops are more or less permanently deployed, and in the late 1960s and early 1970s another conflict on the Korean peninsula appeared a distinct possibility.[8] Prospects for a ½-war contingency in the Persian Gulf region were more or less dismissed until the fall of the Shah of Iran and the Soviet invasion of Afghanistan.

Both the Ford and Carter Administrations endorsed the 1½-war concept as the basis for conventional force planning, although political and budgetary constraints engendered an increasing focus on the "1-war" defense of Europe at the expense of preparations for ½-war contingencies outside the NATO Treaty area. This was especially true of force planning during the Carter Administration, which was determined to rebuild NATO defenses and some of whose officials at times seemed persuaded that the entire Third World was little more than Vietnam writ large—a place in which the United States possessed no vital interests and where, in any event, the direct application of U.S. military power would inevitably entangle the United States in another unwanted conflict. President Carter's proposal of March 1977 to withdraw all remaining U.S. ground combat forces from Korea was but the first of a number of actions that encouraged a relative de-emphasis of naval, amphibious assault, and other categories of conventional forces (including U.S. Army forces forward deployed in Asia) dedicated primarily to potential contingencies beyond a NATO–Warsaw Pact confrontation in Central Europe. Indeed, it is no exaggeration to say that by 1979 the Administration was in actuality pursuing a 1-war strategy, since it had knowingly denied itself the capacity for waging anything more.

A significant feature of the Carter Administration's virtually exclusive planning focus until 1979 on preparation for a war in Europe was an implicit assumption that a war with the Soviet Union in Europe would not extend beyond the North Atlantic area. Until 1979 the prospect of what later became labelled *horizontal escalation*—the spread of combat with Soviet forces beyond a single theater of operations—was more or less ignored, despite the fact that the Soviet Union not only possessed numerically superior ground and tactical air forces in or opposite potential theaters of operations but also enjoyed the advantages of interior lines of communication with respect to simultaneous contingencies (except for the Far East) on the Eurasian landmass. Candid contemplation of the consequences of horizontal escalation undoubtedly was discouraged by the erosion of U.S. military power in Asia, and by the self-imposed budgetary constraints of an administration that came into office pledging to cut defense spending even further than had its predecessor.

To be sure, NATO's defenses were in need of significant repair in the mid-1970s, and the Carter Administration could take credit for a number of initiatives aimed at rebuilding those defenses, including the prepositioning of additional U.S. Army division sets of equipment in Europe, the theater nuclear force modernization program, and the establishment of national defense expenditure goals entailing annual real increases of 3 percent. The price of these and other NATO-related initiatives, however, was a continuing relative decline in U.S. conventional military capabilities dedicated to ½-war contingencies outside the NATO Treaty area.

Indeed, serious doubts persisted as to whether the United States and its NATO allies could prevail even in a "1-war" conflict restricted to Europe alone. The source of those doubts was the dramatic and comprehensive Soviet military buildup that had begun in the late 1960s, when the bulk of U.S. conventional military power was tied down in Southeast Asia. The buildup called into question the viability of NATO's very doctrine of forward defense. The scope of the Soviet buildup, which continued throughout the 1970s, a time of U.S. military retrenchment in Asia and declining annual defense expenditure, was evident in the significant shifts that occurred in the East–West military balance. In the space of little more than a decade following the Soviet invasion of Czechoslovakia in 1968, the Soviet Union managed *simultaneously* to:

1) attain rough parity with the United States in intercontinental nuclear forces;
2) move from a position of inferiority to one of advantage in theater nuclear forces deployed in or targeted on Europe;
3) significantly expand and thoroughly modernize its ground forces deployed in Eastern Europe and Western Russia;

4) transform its tactical air forces (frontal aviation) from a defensive force reliant primarily on short-range interceptors to an offensive force based on long-range, multipurpose aircraft capable of carrying the air war deep into NATO territory;

5) transform its surface navy from what was largely a coastal defense force into a powerful "blue water" force capable of challenging U.S. control of the seas; and

6) eliminate NATO's qualitative advantage in many technologies, especially those associated with land warfare.

An extensive exploration of the changes that have transpired in the military balance since the 1960s is beyond the purview of this study.[9] Suffice it to say, however, that the above developments, in conjunction with declining real U.S. investment in defense, resulted in a sharp decline in U.S. and allied military power in relation to that of the Soviet Union. It was a decline that was not offset by the contraction in U.S. military obligations in Asia, by reversion to a 1½-war criterion for force planning, or by the modest reinvigoration of NATO conventional defenses in the latter 1970s.

In short, although the decade of the 1970s witnessed a substantial reduction in U.S. military aspirations, U.S. military resources dedicated to the fulfillment of those aspirations shrank at a much faster pace relative to the growth of Soviet military power devoted to the denial of those aspirations. The end result was persistence of the wide disparity between U.S. military commitments and resources that first emerged after World War II with the proclamation of the Truman Doctrine. It was a gap reinforced in no small measure by the Nixon Administration's termination of conscription in 1973, and establishment of an All-Volunteer Force capable of recruiting and retaining sufficient manpower only at the price of a deterioration in manpower quality, increased personnel costs as a percentage of U.S. defense expenditure, and a drastic decline in the size and quality of U.S. ground force reserve components essential to Europe's reinforcement.[10] This momentous decision was made for purely political reasons, primary among them being a desire to eliminate campus protest against the Vietnam War.

Responsibility for the decline of U.S. military power in the 1970s vis-à-vis that of the Soviet Union and in relation to American military obligations overseas cannot be confined simply to the combination of Soviet military expansion and an American public and Congress traumatized by Vietnam. The dogged pursuit of comprehensive détente with the Soviet Union by the Nixon, Ford, and (until 1979–1980) Carter Administrations was no less major a factor. Initial expectations about détente—that it would lead to fundamental alterations in Moscow's international behavior conducive to an era of lasting peace, expectations that proved unwarranted but that were deliberately fanned by official Washington—made it all the more difficult to gain public and congressional support for necessary U.S. military responses to the Soviet Union's continuing military buildup.

NOTES

1. Richard M. Nixon, quoted in Kissinger, *The White House Years*, p. 224.
2. Richard M. Nixon, *U.S. Foreign Policy for the 1970s, a New Strategy for Peace* (Washington, D.C.: U.S. Government Printing Office, 1970), pp. 55–56.
3. Gaddis, *Strategies of Containment*, p. 322.
4. Kissinger, *The White House Years*, p. 215.
5. Ibid. p. 221.
6. Ibid. p. 221.
7. Nixon, *U.S. Foreign Policy*, p. 129.
8. Mounting tensions on the Korean peninsula were highlighted by a rising number of bloody incidents along the DMZ, by North Korea's seizure of the *U.S.S. Pueblo* and downing of a U.S. EC-121, and by North Korean attempts to assassinate South Korean President Park Chung Hee.
9. See, for example, Phillip A. Karber, *To Lose An Arms Race: The Competition in Conventional Forces Deployed in Central Europe 1965–1980*, a paper presented at the European American Institute for Security Research, St. Paul de Vence, France, September 17, 1982; Joseph M. A. H. Luns, *NATO and Warsaw Pact Force Comparisons* (NATO, 1982): *Soviet Military Power*, 2nd ed. (Washington, D.C.: Department of Defense, 1983); Donald R. Cotter et al., *The Nuclear "Balance" in Europe: Status, Trends, Implications* (Washington, D.C.: U.S. Strategic Institute, 1983); and the author's *Force Reductions in Europe: Starting Over* (Cambridge, Mass.: Institute for Foreign Policy Analysis, 1980); and *NATO's Theater Force Modernization Program: The Real Issues* (Cambridge, Mass.: Institute for Foreign Policy Analysis, 1981).
10. See, for example, Kenneth J. Coffey, *Strategic Implications of the All-Volunteer Force: The Conventional Defense of Europe* (Chapel Hill: University of North Carolina Press, 1979).

CHAPTER 4

THE CARTER DOCTRINE, RAPID DEPLOYMENT FORCE, AND WORLDWIDE WAR STRATEGY, 1979–PRESENT

In 1979 there occurred three events that provoked a dramatic reinflation of U.S. military aspirations, reversing the trend of the post-Vietnam era. The first was the highly publicized Senate debate on the ratification of the SALT II Treaty, a debate that culminated in 1979 and ended with the Carter Administration's withdrawal of the treaty following the Soviet invasion of Afghanistan. The debate revealed to both the Congress and the American public the degree to which U.S. military power had been permitted to deteriorate in the face of an unstinting and comprehensive Soviet military buildup. From that debate emerged the beginnings of a new national consensus on the need to rebuild U.S. military power, a consensus that in the early 1980s was successfully translated by the Reagan Administration into substantial real increases in defense spending.

The second event was the overthrow of the Shah of Iran by a xenophobic, anti-Western movement composed largely of fanatic Islamic fundamentalists. The collapse of America's chief military client in the Persian Gulf not only removed a major front-line military prop in the region upon which the United States depended heavily for the defense of shared interests in Southwest Asia; it also brought home the degree to which continued Western access to vital oil supplies in the Persian Gulf could be swiftly jeopardized by unexpected political events in the region over which the United States could not hope to exercise any real control. The subsequent seizure of U.S. diplomatic personnel as hostages in Tehran further underscored America's vulnerability and helplessness.

The greatest casualty was not the Shah's regime but rather the Nixon Doctrine, the essence of which was the substitution, where possible, of indigenous allied military manpower and conventional forces for U.S. military power. Iran under the Shah was a showcase of the Nixon Doctrine: a regime that, in exchange for the requisite security assistance and U.S. commitment to its survival, was prepared to defend shared interests, thereby relieving the United States of the costly burden of having to "conceive all the plans, design all the programs, execute all the decisions and undertake all the defense of the free nations of the world."[1] The fall of the Shah advertised the potential vulnerability of Nixon Doctrine client

states to popular hostility stemming in part from an intimate strategic association
with the United States.

The third and perhaps most significant event of 1979 was the Soviet Union's
invasion of Afghanistan in December. The invasion came as a decided shock to
the Carter Administration, provoking a reappraisal of official assumptions about
Soviet motives and methods in the international arena. The result of that reappraisal
was the proclamation of what became known as the Carter Doctrine. The President,
in his January 20, 1980, State of the Union address, declared that

> . . . any attempt by any outside force to gain control of the Persian Gulf region
> will be regarded as an assault on the vital interests of the United States of America,
> and such an assault will be repelled by any means necessary, including military
> force.

The Carter Doctrine for the first time formally committed U.S. military power
to the defense of Southwest Asia: a huge, distant, logistically remote region of
the world in which the United States did not then and does not now enjoy the
enormous operational benefits of politically secure military access ashore in
peacetime. In so doing, the Carter Doctrine imposed new and exceedingly difficult
obligations on U.S. conventional forces already severely overtaxed by traditional
commitments in Europe and the Far East.

To be sure, U.S. military interest in the Persian Gulf region long antedated
the Carter Doctrine. As early as 1949 a U.S. Middle East Force was established,
consisting of naval units operating out of the Persian Gulf, and for the next three
decades U.S. carrier battlegroups made their presence felt in the region on various
occasions, notably during the Indo-Pakistani crisis that occurred during the Nixon
Administration. Not until the Carter Doctrine, however, was U.S. military power
committed so emphatically and indiscriminately to the region's defense.

In an attempt to provide the Doctrine some military teeth, the Administration
accelerated the establishment of the Rapid Deployment Joint Task Force (RDJTF,
subsequently renamed the U.S. Central Command), a new headquarters charged
with identifying, training, and planning the employment of units suitable for
rapid deployment to Southwest Asia. Related initiatives included budget requests
for specialized logistics ships and more strategic transport aircraft and negotiations
with several countries in the Gulf region for contingent access to military facilities.[2]

Paradoxically, however, the Administration requested no significant increases
in conventional force levels. The decision was made instead to form the RDJTF
from units already in the force structure, almost all of which were earmarked
for the defense of Europe or the Far East. It was believed that extant forces
could do the job if properly restructured and re-equipped and provided the means
of getting to the Gulf when needed.

The implications of that decision were profound, especially in light of the fact
that the Carter Doctrine was directed primarily against further overt *Soviet* aggression

in Southwest Asia. In circumstances involving a U.S.–Soviet confrontation in the region, the strategic risk of U.S. reliance on forces committed to both Gulf and NATO contingencies is obvious, given the Soviet Union's possession of interior lines of communication, larger forces, and greater proximity to both Europe and the Gulf.

The mismatch between obligations and resources symbolized by a Persian Gulf intervention force composed of units committed to contingencies elsewhere was not lost upon the Pentagon and the defense intellectual community. In 1980 Under Secretary of Defense (Research and Development) William Perry noted that "the really troublesome problem we have is how do we accommodate [a] NATO buildup and the Persian Gulf buildup at the same time? That is the rub."[3] Army Chief of Staff Edward C. Meyer stated flatly that U.S. conventional force levels were "not sufficient to repel a Soviet assault [in the Persian Gulf] without jeopardizing our NATO commitment."[4] Chief of Naval Operations Thomas B. Hayward testified that his "1½-ocean navy" could not meet the "three-ocean commitment" imposed by the Carter Doctrine.[5] Congressional military analyst John Collins wrote that

> . . . our active status strategic reserves are too few to fight even a modest war in the Middle East without accepting calculated risks that uncover crucial interests elsewhere. Even "best case" forces would probably prove insufficient against the Soviets, whose ability to project offensive power beyond their frontiers has improved impressively in recent years.[6]

And Senator William Cohen, Chairman of the Senate Armed Services Subcommittee on Sea Power and Force Projection, cautioned that

> . . . it is difficult to envisage any major shooting war between the United States and the Soviet Union confinable to the Gulf alone. In all probability such a conflict would spill over into at least the European theater, raising the grim prospect of war on two strategically independent fronts against an adversary possessing superior forces on both, and enjoying the advantage of interior lines of communication.[7]

When the Carter Administration left office in 1981, it thus left behind a gap between U.S. military aspirations and resources as wide as that which plagued the Kennedy and Johnson Administrations. It was an imbalance that was largely self-inflicted, the product of a refusal to match new military obligations, deliberately undertaken, with appropriate increases in conventional force levels. A new headquarters and planned increases in the strategic mobility of U.S. ground and tactical air forces proved no substitute for the real additional military muscle needed to defend U.S. interests in Southwest Asia without endangering the ability of the United States to deliver on its longstanding commitments in Europe and the Far East.

Some Carter Administration officials have argued that the Carter Doctrine did not dictate a commensurate expansion in U.S. conventional force levels, since its purpose was simply to put the Soviet Union on notice that the United States regarded Southwest Asia as vital to its own security, and would be prepared to respond to further Soviet aggression in the region with possible military action in other areas of the world where the regional military balance was more favorable to the United States. Former National Security Advisor Zbigniew Brzezinski has compared the Carter Doctrine to the Truman Doctrine, noting that

. . . President Truman also did not have the capacity to match the Soviets man for man or tank for tank either in Greece or, a year or so later, in Berlin, where he responded firmly to the threat. The point of both the Truman Doctrine and . . . the Carter Doctrine was to make the Soviet Union aware of the fact that the intrusion of Soviet armed forces into an area of vital importance to the United States would precipitate an engagement *with* the United States, and that the United States would be free to choose the manner in which it would respond. In fact, in our private contingency preparations, I made the point of instructing the Defense Department to develop options involving both "horizontal and vertical escalation" in the event of a Soviet move toward the Persian Gulf, by which I meant that we would be free to choose either the terrain or the tactic or the level of our response.[8]

Brzezinski unfortunately fails to note the profoundly different geostrategic environments of the Truman and Carter Doctrines. The former was proclaimed against the backdrop of a U.S. monopoly of nuclear weapons, unchallenged U.S. naval and air supremacy, and a Soviet Union economically prostrate from World War II. Those conditions, all of which had vanished by 1980, afforded the United States a wide freedom of choice with respect to vertical and horizontal responses to Soviet aggression in Europe or Asia.

The incoming Reagan Administration was highly critical of its predecessor's defense policies. Although the Administration, having little choice, more or less endorsed the new U.S. military obligations imposed by the Carter Doctrine, it rejected the proposition that those obligations could be fulfilled by simply tinkering with existing U.S. conventional forces.

Indeed, the Reagan Administration was committed to an across-the-board expansion and modernization of U.S. nuclear and conventional forces, to be financed by major sustained real annual increases in defense expenditure. The Administration was determined to reverse the steady decline of U.S. military power in relation to that of the Soviet Union and to narrowing the yawning abyss separating U.S. military obligations overseas and conventional force levels. The Carter Administration was condemned for having inflated those obligations without appropriate increases in the defense budget while at the same time allowing the U.S. nuclear deterrent to atrophy.

The Carter Administration also was criticized for what many Reagan supporters believed was an excessive force planning focus on the defense of NATO's Central

Front at the expense of preparation for potential contingencies elsewhere. This focus was censured on a number of grounds, including its highly questionable implicit assumption that a "1 war" with the Soviet Union in Europe would not spill over into other theaters of operations. Writing in 1980, Francis J. West, Jr., who later served in the Reagan Administration as Assistant Secretary of Defense for International Security Affairs, denounced the very concept of 1½-wars as a basis for force planning:

> It is currently assumed that the "one war" of the "one and a half war" strategy is limited to battle on the Central Front and that the United States can prepare (allocate resources) for that war under the assumption that fighting will not spread to other theaters. NATO forces in the Center Region will be so strong that the Soviets will not have sufficient forces to divert to other theaters. Nor will the Soviets start a war except on the Central Front because, if they do, NATO has the escalation option of initiating conventional war in the Center Region. In such escalation, Soviet forces would be caught out of position and the resultant losses, including portions of Eastern Europe, would not, to the Soviets, be worth gains elsewhere. In other words, the essence of the "one and a half war" strategy . . . is that, if the center is strong, that strength will extend the deterrence of conflict to other regions where the military balance is even less favorable.

> To assume the "one war" will be mutually restricted (by the United States and by the Soviet Union) to the Central Front of Europe is poor strategy and poorer history, given the course of prior world wars. The Central-Front-only strategy is an assumption driven by undue budgetary pressures. To assume that NATO strength on the Central Front can extend deterrence to other theaters is to ignore a decade of trends. The United States, by 1979, had lost the credible threat of escalation dominance. So it was only proper and prudent to build NATO's conventional strength in the Center Region. It was not prudent to assume that this effort . . . spread an umbrella of deterrence over other areas. Soviet strength had grown far too powerful for the United States to regain the 1969 balance of power. It has not been strategically sound to neglect NATO's flanks and to discount U.S. strengths outside NATO's land mass . . . as a means of offsetting some Soviet strengths and NATO weaknesses. In sum, the "one war" concept is restrictive in focus and outdated in its concept of extended deterrence.[9]

Another critic argued that

> . . . our worst condition is a world war involving our allies and ourselves against the Soviets and their allies and clients. The basic question is how widespread this war might become. If it is limited to the NATO theater in Western Europe, this would constitute a one-front war requiring operations only across the Atlantic. If the war spreads to—or grows from—operations bordering *either* the Pacific or the Indian Ocean, then we would have a two-front war to cope with. If the war spreads to—or grows from—both the Pacific and the Indian Ocean areas, then we would need a three-front capability to cope. In the not too distant future we may even need to consider a fourth front—in the Caribbean and Central America.

If one believes that the Soviets plan direct aggression into Western Europe and are willing to take the consequences of its destruction in the process, then one might be willing to plan on a one-front war in the NATO theater. If, on the other hand, the Soviets wish the benefits of Western Europe without destroying it, then they might well try to force the United States to fight elsewhere in the hopes that Western Europe, by intimidation, would collapse without a fight. Given the increasing number of unstable regions in the world and given the continuing spread of Soviet client states, it would appear that they might entrap us in either the Pacific or the Indian Ocean—or both—in the hopes of reducing our deterrent in the NATO area. South Asia could serve that purpose.

With anything less than a three-front capability, we risk the loss of at least one front to save the other one or two. This does not appear to be a very reasonable bargain. Should we lose the Persian Gulf and Middle East to "save" Japan and Korea? Should we lose Japan and Korea—and then quite probably China— to "save" the Persian Gulf? Should we lose Western Europe to "save" the others— or vice versa? How should the question be phrased: can we afford to "save" all three, or can we afford not to "save" all three?[10]

Indeed, a central premise of the Reagan Administration's military strategy is that any shooting war with the Soviet Union, in whatever region of the world it might start, is likely to spread quickly to other theaters of operations:

For many years, it has been U.S. policy to let the investment and planning for our conventional forces be determined primarily by the requirement for fighting a war centered in Europe, and in which NATO forces would be attacked by the Warsaw Pact. This emphasis recognized that Soviet military forces were concentrated in Central Europe. Preoccupation with the need to be strong in the center led to the mistaken assumption that if the Alliance could meet this largest threat, it would meet lesser ones.[11]

We must recognize that the Soviet Union has enough active forces and reserves to conduct simultaneous campaigns in more than one theater. As a result, we must understand that war could spread to other regions.[12]

A corollary assumption is that other nations hostile to the United States might seek to take advantage of the United States during such a conflict, opening up additional fronts beyond those engaging U.S. and Soviet forces. Administration officials have argued, for example, that in a NATO–Warsaw Pact conflict, Cuban and Cuban-based Soviet forces would seek to interrupt the flow of U.S. reinforcements to Europe, many of which are slated for movement through the Caribbean. Libya, Vietnam, and North Korea also have been cited as potential troublemakers in a worldwide war with the Soviet Union.

The possibility of being confronted by multiple threats simultaneously means that U.S. conventional force planning must reject

. . . the mistaken argument as to whether we should prepare to fight "two wars," "one and a half wars," or some other such tally of wars. Such mechanistic assumptions neglect both the risks and the opportunities that we might confront. We may be forced to cope with Soviet aggression or Soviet-backed aggression, on several fronts.[13]

It also means that U.S. military forces must, in the words of Secretary of Defense Caspar W. Weinberger,

. . . be able to meet the demands of a worldwide war, including concurrent reinforcement of Europe, deployments to Southwest Asia and the Pacific, and support for other areas. . . .

Given the Soviets' ability to launch simultaneous attacks in [Southwest Asia], NATO, and the Pacific, our long-range goal is to be capable of defending all theaters simultaneously.[14]

The objectives of the Administration's "worldwide war" strategy are not confined to those of being able to wage war simultaneously on several fronts. They extend to that of being able to do so for years, if necessary:

Another fallacy in recent defense policy regarding conventional warfare has been the "short war" assumption—the notion that in planning our strategy and designing our forces we could rely on the assumption that a conventional war would be of short duration. Common sense and past experience tell us otherwise. I have therefore instituted changes in our defense policy to correct this fallacy.

It goes without saying that, should our policy to deter aggression fail and conventional conflict be forced upon us, the United States would bend every effort to win the war as quickly as possible. The two wars in which the United States has fought since the beginning of the nuclear era, however, were both of long duration. Unless we are so strong, or our enemy so weak that we could quickly achieve victory, we cannot count on a war ending within a few months.

. . . Deterrence would be weakened if the enemy were misled to believe that he could outlast us in a conventional war. In particular, for a vulnerable and vital region like Southwest Asia, a U.S. strategy that promised our adversaries a "short war" could be an invitation to aggression.[15]

In such a protracted, multifront war, the United States moreover should

. . . not . . . restrict ourselves to meeting aggression on its own immediate front. We might decide to stretch our capabilities, to engage the enemy in many places, or to concentrate our forces and military assets in a few of the most critical arenas.

A wartime strategy that confronts the enemy, were he to attack, with the risk of
our counteroffensive against his vulnerable points strengthens deterrence. . . . Our
counteroffensives should be directed at places where we can affect the outcome of
the war. If it is to offset the enemy's attack, it should be launched against territory
or assets that are of an importance to him comparable to the ones he is attacking.[16]

The "worldwide war" strategy's counteroffensive against the enemy's "vulnerable
points" is exemplified by the Reagan Administration's plans for the U.S. Navy,
which is to be expanded by a margin significantly greater than the other services.
The Administration seeks a 15-carrier battlegroup, 600-ship navy that will "restore
and maintain maritime superiority over the Soviets."[17] This superiority will be
restored and maintained not only through fleet expansion but also through adoption
of a more aggressive war-fighting doctrine. The new doctrine seeks to "prevail"
simultaneously over "the combined military threat of our adversaries" in the
Pacific, Indian, and Atlantic Oceans, including the Norwegian Sea.[18] The Soviet
Navy is not simply to be bottled up in the constrained waters through which it
must pass to reach open ocean; it is to be destroyed at its source through a variety
of measures, including the use of carrier air strikes against ports and naval
installations in the Soviet homeland, even though critics point out that the doctrine could prove prohibitively expensive, since it would require bringing the
carriers into waters infested with Soviet submarines and well within range of
land-based Soviet air power dedicated to the destruction of the U.S. surface
navy.[19] Other critics have expressed concern over the potential effects on escalation
control of even conventional strikes on targets in the Soviet homeland.[20]

The basic force planning hypotheses of the Reagan Administration, at least
in regard to a potential conflict with the Soviet Union, seem eminently prudent
if not unarguable. A U.S.–Soviet war probably would not be confined to Europe
or to any other single theater of operations, and the prospect of other hostile
countries joining in cannot be readily dismissed. Nor are there convincing grounds
for assuming that a war with the Soviet Union would be comparatively short,
despite what would be an inherent and ever-present threat of vertical escalation;
modern history is littered with "short" wars that ended up lasting for years.

Moreover, despite a pronounced emphasis on preparation for contingencies
beyond the North Atlantic Treaty area, including contingencies not involving
hostilities with the Soviet Union, U.S. force deployments and procurement programs
continue to reflect the continuing singular strategic importance of Europe to the
United States. Like its predecessors, the Reagan Administration recognizes that
no area outside North America is as vital to the security and the economic well-
being of the United States. In a worldwide war, Soviet conquest of Europe would
be the decisive event because it would eliminate America's main strategic foothold
on the Eurasian landmass, and could drive both China and remaining U.S. allies
on or along the Eurasian periphery into accommodation with Moscow. While
the Administration is correct in arguing that a strong defense of Europe does

not necessarily "spread an umbrella of deterrence over other areas," it also recognizes that those other areas are not equal to Europe in strategic importance and that they would be all the more difficult to defend in the event of disaster in Europe.

Nor should the Administration's declared commitment to a "concurrent" defense "of Europe . . . Southwest Asia and the Pacific" be misconstrued. Simultaneous engagement of Soviet military power in two or more theaters of operations on or along the Eurasian landmass is not synonymous with equality of military effort in each. U.S. force planners plainly recognize that, given the Soviet Union's geographic and initial operational and force-ratio advantages, the United States almost certainly would be compelled, as it was in World War II, to concentrate its main military effort in certain theaters (as well as in certain areas in each theater) at the expense of others. Some areas—even entire theaters—might have to be written off, at least temporarily. Points of concentration would be determined by defensive priorities and unfolding opportunities presented by inherent Soviet military weaknesses (see discussion in Chapter 8) and by Soviet operational errors. As in World War II, sequential operations would be the order of the day.

Thus, to argue that the Administration's worldwide war strategy would inevitably result in a mindless dispersion of limited U.S. resources in the presence of a larger adversary with better internal lines of communication (at least with respect to conflict waged in Europe and the Persian Gulf) is to presume that U.S. force planners are strategically incompetent. It is also to argue implicitly for a declaratory U.S. strategy that would in effect cede control of one area of the Free World or another to the Soviet Union in advance of hostilities. Needless to say, such a declaratory strategy would have deleterious effects on allied political cohesion and prewar and wartime deterrence, as well as deny the United States potential operational opportunities.

The central problem confronting the Reagan Administration's military strategy is the same problem that has plagued U.S. military strategy since 1945—a peacetime imbalance of ends and means, responsibilities and resources, commitments and capabilities, of a magnitude sufficient to call into question prospects for success in the event of war, and certainly a general war with the Soviet Union waged on two or more major fronts. Whatever may be said about the declared goals of the Administration's strategy, goals which for the most part reflect overseas commitments undertaken by preceding administrations, the stark reality is that the United States, even in conjunction with its allies, does not possess, nor will it in the future, conventional forces sufficient to engage Soviet military power effectively on a global scale in the event of a general war. Senator Sam Nunn has concluded that "[the Reagan Administration's] military strategy far exceeds our present and projected [military] resources,"[21] a judgment that is widely shared within the Pentagon:

> Even an increase in U.S. military investments as high as 14% per year, continued throughout the decade, would not close the gap in accumulated military assets

between the U.S. and Soviet Union until the early 1990s. That is a bleak outlook, implying either further deterioration in our security or a need for a defense increase considerably steeper than what the Administration now proposes.[22]

We are accepting tremendous risks with the size of forces that we have to do what we have pledged to do.[23]

The magnitude of the mismatch is reflected in the huge disparity between extant and projected conventional force levels, on the one hand, and those believed by the Joint Chiefs of Staff to be necessary to provide reasonable assurance of fulfilling the objectives of the "worldwide war" strategy on the other. In 1982 the JCS recommended conventional force levels that would have cost up to $750 billion more than the $1.6 trillion requested in the Administration's Fiscal Year 1982 Five-Year Defense Plan, which itself represented a major increase in U.S. defense expenditure over that of previous years.[24]

In 1983, during preparation of the Fiscal Year 1985–1989 Defense Guidance, the JCS recommended, again unsuccessfully, large increases in the numbers of active-duty ground force divisions, carrier battlegroups, Air Force fighter wings, and long-range air transports.[25] Table 3 shows the differences between these forces on hand in 1983, planned for 1989, and recommended for 1989 by the JCS. What is immediately striking is how little the Reagan Administration is actually buying in the way of additional conventional forces, notwithstanding its success in obtaining significant real increases in defense expenditure. The Administration plans to add but one division to the Army's present force of 16 divisions, despite the fact that at least four additional Army divisions would be required to permit that service to fulfill its responsibilities in Southwest Asia without jeopardizing its ability to reinforce Europe as planned.[26] The Air Force is to receive only three new tactical fighter wings, and less than 50 additional long-range air transports for a total of 348, despite the Pentagon's assessment

TABLE 3. Proposed U.S. Conventional Force Level Increases, 1983–1989

CATEGORY OF FORCE	FORCES ON HAND 1983	FORCES PLANNED BY DOD FOR 1989	FORCES RECOMMENDED FOR 1989 BY JCS
Active army divisions	16	17	23
Marine amphibious forces	3	3	4
Navy carrier battle groups	13	15	24
Air Force fighter wings	24	27	44
Long-range air transports	304	348	1,308

Source: Richard Halloran, "New Weinberger Directive Refines Military Policy," *New York Times* (March 22, 1983).

that almost four times that many are needed to meet the acute strategic mobility requirements even of a sequentially conducted multifront worldwide war. As in the 1960s and 1970s, strategic mobility requirements are once again being short-changed. One prominent defense analyst has concluded that

> . . . lack of enough strategic mobility is probably the single greatest flaw in our conventional force posture. . . . We have today in the continental United States more ready active forces than we can deploy rapidly enough to meet immediate strategic needs—a seriously unbalanced force posture. While the Reagan Administration is expanding air and sealift . . . what is being done is far short of what is needed.[27]

The Navy is to receive two more carrier battlegroups for a total of 15, although the JCS has postulated a budgetarily unconstrained requirement of 24 groups. Even the goal of a 600-ship navy now appears to be in some jeopardy, what with spiraling unit costs and mounting congressional opposition, short-sighted or not, to sustaining annual real increases in the defense budget averaging 9.2 percent[28] in the face of massive federal deficits. In all likelihood, however, the 600-ship goal will be achieved, since most of the contracts necessary to reach that goal already have been let, and the price of cancellation would equal or exceed the costs of going ahead with the program.

There is in fact no assurance that the Congress, which more often than not has exhibited an unwillingness to address fully and act upon the budgetary implications of adverse shifts in the East–West military balance in the last fifteen years, will fully fund the conventional force level increases proposed in the Administration's Five-Year Defense Plan. In 1983 the Congress slashed from 10.5 percent to 5.0 percent the real defense spending increase requested for fiscal year 1984.

Even were the Congress to accede fully to the Administration's request, it is doubtful whether the Five-Year Plan contains sufficient money even to finance anticipated increases in U.S. conventional force levels.[29] No less questionable is whether the All-Volunteer Force could adequately man those force levels, especially in an environment of economic recovery that substantially reduced levels of unemployment. Even in such an environment, the All-Volunteer Force in the coming decade will still confront a continuing absolute and relative decline in the size of the 19-year-old American male population, which will shrink from 2,086,000 in 1983 to 1,622,000 by 1993.

In short, notwithstanding the Reagan Administration's determined and partially successful efforts to bring U.S. military power into closer alignment with U.S. military commitments abroad (most of which, with the prominent exceptions of Lebanon and Grenada, the Administration inherited), the gap between U.S. military responsibilities and resources remains—and is likely to remain—dangerously wide.

NOTES

1. Nixon, *U.S. Foreign Policy*, p. 6.
2. For a comprehensive discussion and analysis of the Rapid Deployment Joint Task Force and the problems confronting U.S. military power in Southwest Asia, see the author's *The Rapid Deployment Force and U.S. Military Intervention in the Persian Gulf* (Cambridge, Mass.: Institute for Foreign Policy Analysis, 1981).
3. William Perry, *Department of Defense Authorization for Appropriations for Fiscal Year 1981, Hearings before the Committee on Armed Services*, United States Senate, 96th Congress, Second Session (1980), Part 6, p. 3275.
4. Ibid. Part 2, p. 745.
5. Ibid. Part 2, p. 785.
6. John M. Collins et al., *Petroleum Imports from the Persian Gulf: Use of U.S. Armed Force to Ensure Supplies* (Washington, D.C.: Library of Congress Congressional Research Service, 1980), p. 16.
7. William Cohen, *Department of Defense Authorization for Appropriations for Fiscal Year 1982, Hearings before the Committee on Armed Services*, United States Senate, 97th Congress, First Session (1981), Part 4, p. 1700.
8. Zbigniew Brzezinski, *Power and Principle, Memoirs of the National Security Advisor 1977–1981* (New York: Farrar, Straus & Giroux, 1983), p. 445.
9. Francis J. West, Jr., "Conventional Forces Beyond NATO," in W. Scott Thompson, ed., *National Security in the 1980s, From Weakness to Strength* (San Francisco: Institute for Contemporary Studies, 1980), pp. 324, 326–8.
10. Leonard Sullivan, Jr., "Correlating National Security Strategy and Defense Investment," in Thompson, *National Security in the 1980s* p. 347.
11. Caspar W. Weinberger, *Annual Report to the Congress for Fiscal Year 1983* (Washington, D.C.: Department of Defense, 1982), p. I–14.
12. Caspar W. Weinberger, *Annual Report to the Congress for Fiscal Year 1984* (Washington, D.C.: Department of Defense, 1983), p. 35.
13. Weinberger, *Annual Report for Fiscal Year 1983*, p. I–15.
14. Ibid. p. III–91.
15. Ibid. pp. II–16, 17.
16. Ibid. p. II–16.
17. Ibid. p. II–12.
18. Testimony of Secretary of the Navy John Lehman. U.S. Congress, House Committee on Armed Services, *Hearings on the Military Posture and H.R. 5968*, 97th Congress, Second Session, 1982, pp. 561–2.
19. See, for example, Stansfield Turner and George Thibault, "Preparing for the Unexpected: The Need for a New Military Strategy," *Foreign Affairs* (Fall, 1982).
20. Barry R. Posen and Stephen Van Evera, "Defense Policy and the Reagan Administration: Departure from Containment," *International Security* (Summer, 1983).
21. Sam Nunn, speech before the Georgetown Center for Strategic and International Studies, Washington, D.C., March 18, 1983.
22. Statement by Under Secretary of Defense Fred Iklé before the Senate Armed Services Committee, February 26, 1982, p. 3.
23. Testimony of General Edward C. Meyer before the Senate Armed Services Committee, February 2, 1982.
24. George C. Wilson, "U.S. Defense Paper Cites Gap Between Rhetoric, Intentions," *Washington Post* (May 27, 1982).
25. Richard Halloran, "New Weinberger Directive Refines Military Policy," *New York Times* (March 22, 1983).

26. See *Rapid Deployment Forces: Policy and Budgetary Implications* (Washington, D.C.: Congressional Budget Office, 1983).

27. Robert Komer, "Future U.S. Conventional Forces: A Coalition Approach," in *Rethinking Defense and Conventional Forces* (Washington, D.C.: Center for National Policy, 1983), p. 47.

28. As requested in the proposed defense budget for fiscal years 1982–1985.

29. See Kuhn, "Ending Defense Stagnation."

PART II.
HARMONIZING
ASPIRATIONS AND RESOURCES

PART II.
HARMONIZING
ASPIRATIONS AND RESOURCES

The time has come for the United States to develop a new conventional strategy that aligns goals and forces, if for no other reason than to offset the corrosive consequences of the loss of nuclear superiority over the Soviet Union.

Is it possible to bridge the abyss between military obligations and resources that has bedevilled American military strategy since World War II? Can those obligations be brought into line with forces dedicated to their fulfillment without a substantial reduction in treaty commitments, which could drive abandoned allies into accommodation with the Soviet Union? Can aspirations and resources be harmonized without massive, economically debilitating increases in defense expenditure, which are likely to be politically impossible to sustain?

The answer to all three questions is yes. To be sure, the United States has, to paraphrase Lord Palmerston, no perpetual allies or enemies, only a perpetual interest in preventing the domination of the Eurasian landmass by a hostile power. And, to be sure, the United States should assiduously avoid military commitments, such as that of the U.S. Marines in Beirut in 1983–1984, characterized by opaque political objectives and insufficient force. Also to be avoided, as Vietnam demonstrated, are the strategic risks inherent in an indiscriminating application of containment of Communist expansion, especially in places of little intrinsic value to the United States and against opponents enjoying natural geographic and operational advantages. If the present entanglement of the Soviet Union in Afghanistan serves U.S. strategic interests, U.S. entanglement in another "Vietnam" would benefit the Soviet Union. An adversary should not, if possible, be permitted to pick the time and place to fight.

Yet the United States *has* a vital interest in the containment of further Soviet expansion in Europe and the Far East. It has a no-less-vital interest in the preservation of access to the oil and mineral deposits of the Persian Gulf and elsewhere in the Third World. For 40 years the United States has deployed a substantial portion of its ground, naval, and tactical air power abroad, not as an act of charity toward its friends and allies overseas, but rather because forward-deployed forces, in conjunction with a system of alliances designed to enhance U.S. military power, serve the American national interest. It is always better to fight overseas than close to home. Thus to attempt to harmonize U.S. military

49

obligations and resources by cutting the former to fit the latter would be inherently self-defeating. As Robert Komer has trenchantly noted, any new U.S. military strategy "must be based squarely on *America's greatest remaining strategic advantage over the Soviet Union—that we are blessed with many rich allies while the USSR has only a few poor ones*, most of them a strain on the Soviet exchequer."[1] Neither the nostalgic allure of Fortress America nor understandable frustration over many issues related to intra-alliance burden-sharing should be permitted to cloud the inescapable reality of U.S. dependence on *coalition* warfare.

And, to be sure, no new U.S. military strategy based on a reasonable harmony of ends and means can be obtained without sustained real increases in the U.S. defense budget. An effective response to two decades of relentless Soviet military expansion cannot be had on the cheap. The United States can no longer afford, as it did in the 1970s, to finance uncontrolled growth of domestic social and economic welfare programs through declining real defense expenditure.

What follows is an outline and discussion of a proposed new military strategy for the United States. The strategy is designed to meet the following criteria:

1) effective containment of further Soviet military expansion on or along the periphery of the Eurasian landmass, with highest priority assigned to the defense of Europe, Northeast Asia, and the Persian Gulf, in that order;
2) discriminating and sequential engagement of Soviet military power based on a combination of the above strategic priorities and deliberate exploitation of already identifiable Soviet military weaknesses as well as those that might emerge in the course of hostilities;
3) a more rational and militarily effective reallocation of military labor among the United States and its principal allies along functional and geographic lines; and,
4) avoidance of dependence on nuclear weapons as a substitute for conventional forces.

As strategic objectives, the above criteria are certainly not new. Every U.S. administration since 1961 (including the Reagan Administration) has in one fashion or another pursued all four objectives. The same may be said of the substance, if not the detail, of many of the author's specific proposals—the subject of the remaining chapters of this study—for bringing U.S. military obligations into reasonable harmony with capabilities.

NOTE

1. Robert Komer, "Future U.S. Conventional Forces: A Coalition Approach," in *Rethinking Defense and Conventional Forces* (Washington, D.C.: Center for National Policy, 1983), p. 44.

CHAPTER 5.
REALITIES AND OPPORTUNITIES

Any strategy must be predicated on recognition of geostrategic realities and opportunities. As the United States enters the mid-1980s it faces a number of realities and opportunities bearing directly on any attempt to bring its military obligations and power into closer alignment.

The first is that the credibility of threatened or actual nuclear responses to non-nuclear Soviet or Soviet-sponsored aggression has sharply diminished (although certainly not vanished) and is not likely to be restored. Soviet attainment of intercontinental nuclear parity and theater nuclear advantage, by eliminating the ability of the United States to dominate the escalation of conflict across the nuclear threshold, has placed a premium on the ability to defeat non-nuclear aggression without a resort to nuclear fire. As noted by NATO's former commander of the Central Front:

> For far too long, the Atlantic Alliance has accepted gaps and weaknesses in its military potential and has contented itself with the idea that they would be offset by superiority in other fields. To put it more bluntly, the Western alliance has grown accustomed to living with the massive conventional superiority of the Warsaw Pact forces—a situation that has existed for a long time and that has been worsening consistently in recent years. In the last analysis, the Alliance has relied upon the deterrent effect of the superior American strategic nuclear potential.

> The era of American strategic nuclear superiority, however, is over forever. Given this fact, disequilibriums below the level of strategic nuclear weapons, not only in the Warsaw Pact's conventional superiority but also in the Soviet's superiority in intermediate-range nuclear weapons, become much more significant. Counterforces sufficient to match each segment of a potential offensive have become indispensable. The defenders must possess the means to meet an aggressor in such a manner as to make initiation or continuation of a conflict involve unacceptably high risks for the attacker. For this reason, a conventional defense capability is required.[1]

The growing nonutility of nuclear weapons in conflicts between nuclear-armed states or alliances does not mean that they have lost all value. Parity serves to deter both sides from initiating nuclear fire, and the very presence of nuclear weapons on the battlefield, especially if governed—as are NATO's theater forces—by a doctrine of calculated ambiguity with respect to the circumstances in which

51

they might be used, serves to complicate the operational planning of a potential aggressor. For example, the mere prospect that nuclear weapons might come into play in a conflict in Europe compels attacking Soviet forces to disperse, thus denying them the benefits of concentration historically associated with successful blitzkrieg. Nuclear deterrence makes conventional defense less difficult.

For these and other reasons it is imperative that the United States and its European allies continue to modernize their intercontinental and theater nuclear forces while at the same time creating a credible conventional deterrent. Barring an acceptable arms control alternative, NATO should proceed to implement fully its decision of December 12, 1979, to modernize its intermediate-range theater nuclear forces, and the United States should proceed to modernize its intercontinental nuclear forces. NATO also should refrain from discarding its longstanding doctrine of first use of theater nuclear weapons. Incredible though its actual application might be in the face of the Soviet Union's mounting theater nuclear advantage in Europe (and NATO's own tortuous nuclear release procedures), the doctrine of first use unquestionably heightens the uncertainties confronting Pact force planners, who could never be sure that NATO would not resort to nuclear fire first. It is, in any event, bad strategy to inform a potential adversary in advance of what you will not do in the event of war. It is further to be noted that implicit in the doctrine of first use is the assumption that NATO will never start a war in Europe, which makes it difficult to place NATO and Soviet weapons on a morally, politically, or militarily equal plane. The Soviets alone are capable of initiating offensive military action in Europe.

Nor does nuclear stalemate mean that the United States and its allies must match Soviet conventional forces man for man, tank for tank, plane for plane, and ship for ship. It is neither desirable nor necessary to do so. Stalemate does place a premium, however, on retaining—and accelerating—U.S. and allied qualitative advantages over the Soviet Union in critical military technologies, manpower, and training. It also demands war-fighting doctrines designed to exploit Soviet geographic and operational weaknesses while at the same time avoiding, where possible, head-on collisions with Soviet strengths. Since the days of Alexander the Great the history of warfare has repeatedly demonstrated that it is possible to fight outnumbered and win. The key is the ability to substitute brains for brawn.

The second reality is that the locus and character of the Soviet threat to the West have registered significant changes in the last 35 years. From 1949, the year in which NATO was founded, until the early 1960s the principal threat to Western security was perceived to be an overt Soviet invasion of Central Europe. The establishment in Europe of a major, more or less permanent U.S. force presence in the early 1950s was based on this perception of the threat. Preparation for conflict in Europe against first-line Soviet forces continues to drive the size and structure of NATO's general purpose forces and has in the past served to inhibit both U.S. and allied responses to threats outside the Treaty area. The limited nature of U.S. military objectives in the Korean War stemmed in large measure from fear that the initial North Korean invasion was but a feint designed to divert U.S. military resources away from an impending Soviet move against Europe. U.S. force deployments to Southeast Asia in the 1960s were similarly constrained for fear of "uncovering" NATO. And U.S. military responses to the multiple crises that occurred in Southwest Asia in 1979–1980 were enfeebled because of a post-Vietnam force planning focus on strengthening the U.S. commitment to NATO at the expense of preparation for conflict outside Europe.

While the possibility of overt Soviet aggression in Europe cannot be dismissed entirely, it is no longer the only or the most likely Soviet threat to Western security. As former Secretary of Defense James R. Schlesinger has observed, in 1949

> . . . we needed to protect the land mass of Western Europe against the possibility of Soviet invasion and to provide for the recovery of Western Europe. Those requirements were met through the creation of NATO and the Marshall Plan. Today, the security problem has taken on an altered form. The easiest route to the domination of Western Europe by the Soviet Union is through the Persian Gulf. And it is to be noted that NATO is a defensive alliance. It cannot in terms of its own charter respond to what may be the more serious threat against security of Western Europe.[2]

It can be argued that NATO's very success in deterring a direct Soviet frontal assault in Europe has served to channel Soviet expansionism into an alternative, indirect approach aimed at gaining a stranglehold on the economic foundations of Western security. This could be the common denominator of Soviet and Soviet-sponsored violence in Central America, Angola, Ethiopia, Yemen, Iran, Afghanistan, and Indochina. It may account in part for the steady and impressive growth in the size and capabilities of Soviet surface naval, amphibious assault, airlift, airborne, and other force projection capabilities; and in the establishment of Soviet-controlled military bases astride the West's economic lines of communication with the Third World. The Soviet approach is geographically indirect because it focuses on regions outside the NATO Treaty area; it is instrumentally indirect because it relies less upon the direct application of Soviet military power than on local or imported surrogate forces dedicated to the exploitation of political and military instability prevalent in the Third World.

This shift in the locus and character of the Soviet threat does not mean that the United States and its NATO allies can relax their guard in Europe. Although quiescent, Europe remains the center of East–West military confrontation. NATO is, in any event, ill-suited as a vehicle for the collective defense of Western interests outside the Treaty area.

What it does suggest is the need for a larger force presence outside the Treaty area on the part of the United States and those of its allies that are able and willing to contribute to such a presence. It also suggests, given the lack of secure

U.S. and allied military access ashore in peacetime in Southwest Asia and many other critical areas of the Third World, the need for enhanced investment in strategic mobility and sea-based force projection capabilities; and, given the largely indirect character of the Soviet threat there, increased emphasis on special operations forces and on the creation of reliable and competent indigenous client forces.

The third—and closely related—reality is that the United States and its allies no longer enjoy uncontested superiority at sea. In contrast to the geographically compact and relatively autarkic Warsaw Pact, NATO is an alliance of trading nations bifurcated by 3,000 miles of ocean and vitally dependent upon access to distant overseas raw materials. For NATO, maritime superiority is not simply desirable, it is imperative. The Soviet navy's growing ability to interdict, if only temporarily, U.S. and allied maritime lines of communication with the resource-rich Third World is also an ability to interrupt the flow of transatlantic military reinforcements to Europe in the event of war.

In terms of individual ship survivability and fighting power, NATO continues to possess a substantial margin of superiority over the Warsaw Pact, and unlike the Soviet Union, NATO enjoys easy access to the open ocean. On the other hand, the wartime tasks of the Soviet navy would be comparatively simple and less demanding. Denying control of the seas traditionally has been less demanding than gaining or maintaining it, especially if one enjoys, as does the Soviet Union, a preponderance in such sea denial capabilities as mine warfare vessels and attack submarines.

The fourth reality is that the fundamental antagonism between the two largest communist powers in the world is almost certain to persist, barring a breakdown in Sino-American relations. The evolution of China from an ally to an enemy of the Soviet Union is one of the seminal international geostrategic events of the past 30 years, affording the West enormous potential opportunities. By compelling the Soviet Union to deploy approximately one-third of its standing ground, naval, and tactical air forces to the Far East, China has made an immeasurable, albeit indirect, contribution to the military welfare of the United States and its European allies. For the first time in over 40 years Russian force planners, historically paranoid about the dangers of a two-front war, must again contemplate the real prospect of a war in Europe and a war in the Far East against an Asian foe. By her very presence along the Soviet border, even a China not allied to any other major power, hostile to the Soviet Union, and even lacking modern conventional forces capable of mounting anything more than shallow local attacks has fundamentally altered the global geostrategic equation.

Whether the shared strategic interest of the United States and China in containing further Soviet expansion on the Eurasian landmass can and should be translated eventually into an explicit, comprehensive military relationship remains to be seen, and will be discussed in Chapter 7.

Short of war, no conceivable event could so endanger Western security interests as a Sino-Soviet rapprochement that effectively eliminated China as a potential military foe of the U.S.S.R. Such a rapprochement could be as strategically disastrous for the Western democracies as was the Nazi–Soviet Pact of 1939, which by eliminating the threat to Germany in the East gave Hitler a free hand in the West.

The fifth reality is the continuing shift of power *within* the Western alliance. If U.S. military power has suffered a relative decline vis-à-vis that of the Soviet Union, the economic, actual military, and potential military power of Western Europe has risen substantially in relation to that of the United States. In 1949 the United States possessed a practical nuclear monopoly, accounted for over one-half of the world's production and ruled the world's oceans. Europe, still prostrate from World War II, was incapable of meeting even minimal requirements for its own defense. It was against this backdrop that the decision was made to establish a major U.S. force presence in Europe, the principal purpose of which was to provide a military shield behind which Europe, assisted by the Marshall Plan, could recover and eventually, it was assumed (or at least hoped), shoulder the burden for its own conventional forward defense.

Europe's complete recovery and subsequent economic expansion is evident today in a population base, aggregate gross national product, and share of the world's trade larger than those of the United States, whose relative economic power has declined steadily since the late 1940s. Indeed, by the early 1980s the per capita gross national product of several NATO allies had pulled abreast of, or even surpassed that of the United States.

Despite this profound shift in the distribution of economic power within the West, however, the United States continues to bear a disproportionate share of the common military burden. During the period 1971–1980, for example, the United States accounted for 65 percent of the total national defense expenditures of NATO members and maintained 45 percent of the Alliance's total active-duty military personnel, even though the American GNP and population represented but 46 and 38 percent, respectively, of NATO's as a whole.[3] In terms of defense expenditures per capita and as a percentage of GNP the disproportionality became even more pronounced in the early 1980s, as the Reagan Administration initiated its rearmament program against a backdrop of declining allied real increases in annual military outlays. Even in terms of the ratio between military personnel on active duty and total eligible males, only the poorly equipped, conscripted armies of Greece and Turkey are proportionally larger than the U.S. All-Volunteer Force. In short, "we appear to be perpetuating a burden-sharing relationship which was probably appropriate in the 1950s, but which has become unbalanced as other western economies have grown relative to our own."[4]

To be sure, the United States is the only member of the Western alliance that has truly global military responsibilities, and the United States has willingly borne virtually the entire burden of intercontinental and theater nuclear deterrence. It can, moreover, be convincingly argued that many European members of NATO get more for their money than does the United States, in part because of lower personnel costs associated with conscription. The Germany army, for example, whose quality is second to none in the Alliance, fields a total of 12 divisions from an active-duty end-strength of 335,000 personnel, compared to a U.S. Army of 791,000 people and but 16 divisions.

Yet few would argue that the U.S. defense of critical regions outside the Treaty area does not benefit Europe. A free and independent Japan, and unimpeded access to Persian Gulf oil and Third World minerals are as essential to Europe's well-being as they are to that of the United States. The present burden-sharing relationship also is incompatible with the task of countering the Soviet Union's relentless and ongoing military buildup, a task that will require, among other things, allied assumption of military responsibilities more commensurate with their economic strength.

Finally, it should be recognized that the present burden-sharing relationship also has contributed in large measure to mounting public and congressional pressures for unilateral troop withdrawals from Europe, which, if actually undertaken, could threaten the political and military integrity of NATO. The issue of burden-sharing is as much a political as it is a military one. Thus, allied assumption of military responsibilities more commensurate with their economic strength would not only go a long way in producing a reasonable harmonization of U.S. (and NATO) military aspirations and resources but also would defuse a potentially fatal political crisis within the Alliance.

Indeed, in combination, the relative shift of economic and potential military power within the West and the emergence of new threats to shared interests in regions of the world that can be most effectively defended by the United States suggest that a new division of military labor between the United States and its NATO allies is not just desirable but imperative.

This and other means of restoring a proper balance between U.S. military obligations and power is the subject of the following chapters.

NOTES

1. Franz-Joseph Schulze, "Improving Our Conventional Defense," *AEI Foreign Policy and Defense Review*, 4:3/4 (March, 1983), p. 33.
2. James R. Schlesinger, "The Geopolitics of Energy," *The Washington Quarterly* (Summer, 1979), p. 7.
3. Jeffrey Record and Robert J. Hanks, *U.S. Strategy at the Crossroads: Two Views* (Cambridge, Mass.: Institute for Foreign Policy Analysis, 1982), p. 6.
4. Leonard Sullivan, Jr., "The Real Long-Range Defense Dilemma: Burden Sharing," *Armed Forces Journal* (October, 1981), p. 56.

CHAPTER 6.
A NEW TRANSATLANTIC
DIVISION OF MILITARY LABOR

The task of devising a new military strategy that would provide a reasonable harmonization of ends and means, within the framework of present U.S. military obligations overseas and resources likely to be available to U.S. force planners, is not an easy one. It is not, however, an insurmountable one.

The United States and its NATO and Far Eastern allies collectively possess economic power vastly superior to that of the Warsaw Pact, and in fact maintain larger standing ground, naval, and tactical air forces than the Pact. The issue has always been whether the West could translate its advantage in raw economic and military power into effective containment of Soviet expansion on the Eurasian landmass.

The central position of the Warsaw Pact on the Eurasian landmass confers important military advantages upon the Soviet Union, advantages that are further and significantly enhanced by NATO's purely defensive doctrine, which cedes to the Soviet Union in advance the inestimable operational advantages associated with the initiation of hostilities. Modern weaponry and operational doctrines have markedly increased the traditional military benefits of surprise attack against an unready defender.[1] Confidence in the ability of sophisticated surveillance technologies to provide early, unambiguous warning of an impending blow ignores major improvements in means of deception. Even more important, there can be no assurance that political decision-makers will act effectively and in time upon whatever warning is received.

Western defenses along the periphery of Eurasia, from Norway to Korea, also lack great depth, which, operationally, means the ability to trade substantial space for time. Yet the history of modern, mechanized warfare has shown that both the capacity and willingness of a defender to trade space for time is essential in defeating an attack preceded by little or no warning and characterized by rapid, deep thrusts by large concentrations of armor. The success of the German blitzkriegs against the relatively shallow states of Central and Western Europe in 1939–1940 could not be repeated in the vast expanses of Russia against an opponent able and prepared to retreat over a thousand kilometers. The distance from the inter-German border to Antwerp is less than 500 kilometers, and that from Panmunjom to Pusan less than 400 kilometers.

Western fighting power is, moreover, far more dispersed than that of the Warsaw Pact. The most powerful member of the Western alliance and its principal source of reinforcements is separated from the West's front-line defenses in Eurasia by thousands of miles of water, distances that are operationally magnified by chronic shortages in strategic mobility. The combination of comparatively dispersed forces and an exclusively defensive doctrine dilutes the potential of Western military power by reducing the amount that otherwise could be brought immediately to bear in a specific place.

But perhaps the greatest diluent of the potential effectiveness of Western military power is the character of the Western Alliance itself. Unlike the Warsaw Pact, NATO is a voluntary association of sovereign, independent states possessing different perspectives on national and Alliance security needs. Without for a moment suggesting that NATO ought to be anything else, it must be recognized that NATO's character does not promote consensus on the nature of the Soviet threat or the best means of dealing with it. And, in fact, there is little consensus within the Alliance today on either matter, especially between the United States and some of its European allies.

The problem is compounded by the fact that U.S. and European security interests are not and can never be identical as long as the Alliance remains bifurcated by 3,000 miles of water. Europe, confronting Soviet military power on its very doorstep, has a profound stake in deterrence based on the threat of immediate U.S. nuclear retaliation against the Soviet Union itself. To Europeans, an East–West conflict waged high above European territory is infinitely preferable to one waged on it. In contrast is distant America, whose borders are threatened only by penniless refugees and work-hungry Mexicans, and whose force planners understandably view Europe as only one—albeit the most critical—of several potential theaters of military operations. U.S. force planners have a no less profound stake in preventing any conflict in Europe from escalating into an intercontinental nuclear exchange. If war is to be waged, it is always preferable to wage it on someone else's territory. The rub is that there is no Group of Soviet Forces Canada or Group of Soviet Forces Mexico directly threatening the United States.

Nor does the character of NATO promote rationalization of military roles and missions, standardization of weaponry and operational doctrines, or interoperability among national field forces. The costs of national sovereignty in terms of collective military efficiency and effectiveness are persistently evident in unnecessary redundancy and duplication of effort and in an ongoing failure to exploit fully the benefits of natural national military advantage.

The Alliance's virtually exclusive, if understandable, focus on deterrence further dilutes the potential operational effectiveness of its military forces. A good example is the distribution of the various national military contingents in Germany:

The significance of the stationing of troops from six allied nations on German soil (along with the forces of the Federal Republic) . . . is achieved by assigning to the forces of each nation a defense sector running from west to east and ending on the Warsaw Pact border. The plan can best be pictured as a "layer cake" whereby, from north to south, each army corps represents a "layer." The three German corps constitute layers in the northern, central, and southern parts of the Federal Republic. They are thus always ranged with allied corps. Beyond question, such a system has operational disadvantages. It lacks flexibility and operational interchangeability, and above all it creates logistical problems. But the advantages with respect to deterrence outweigh them. A military advance by Warsaw Pact forces in central Europe would no longer constitute an attack on the forces of a single country, but would from the beginning come up against the forces of several allies, including the United States and Great Britain, and involve them in the fighting. This defense plan bolsters the cohesion of mutual defense. It is at once the consequence and the guarantee of solidarity within the alliance.[2]

What follows is not a detailed prescription for a new military strategy for the United States and its allies, complete with operational plans and estimated costs, but rather an attempt to identify the basic elements of a strategy that would bring U.S. (and NATO) military aspirations and resources into reasonable alignment. Those elements include:

1) a new division of military labor within the Western alliance;
2) a more intimate strategic engagement of China;
3) a more deliberate application of Western strengths against Soviet weaknesses;
4) enhanced reliance on reserve forces; and
5) enhanced investment in strategic mobility.

Since NATO's inception, there has always been a rough, informal division of labor among its members, some of which have tended to specialize in areas of natural military advantage. As the economically most powerful and most technologically proficient member of the Alliance, the United States has assumed virtually the entire burden for intercontinental and theater nuclear deterrence, and continues to provide a disproportionate share of NATO's high-performance tactical aircraft and large naval vessels. Moreover, with the demise of European colonial empires in the 1960s, the United States became the only member of the Alliance possessing extensive military obligations overseas and deploying significant forces outside the Treaty area. These obligations, coupled with a commitment to provide substantial reinforcements to NATO early on in a crisis or war, are reflected in a major investment in force projection and strategic mobility that has no parallel in Europe. There is no European equivalent of the *Nimitz*-class aircraft carrier, the B-52 bomber, the C-5 strategic air transport, the United States Marine Corps, or the U.S. Army's 18th Airborne Corps.

To be sure, all armed members of the Alliance[3] maintain naval and tactical air forces, and, in the cases of Great Britain and France, modest nuclear deterrents and not insignificant force projection capabilities. Most European members of NATO, however, have focused their military efforts primarily on the provision of ground forces and supporting tactical aviation (short-range interceptor and close air support aircraft) dedicated to the initial defense of their territory. In Germany, the fulcrum of NATO's doctrine of forward defense, particular emphasis has been accorded by the *Bundeswehr* and by the six other countries deploying ground forces in Germany (including the United States and France) to relatively costly heavy ground forces—armored, armored cavalry, and mechanized infantry formations—which are regarded as essential in dealing effectively with an attack by the Soviet Army, all but eight of whose 187 divisions are also heavy.[4]

Europe's comparative military emphasis on the land battle is certainly understandable, given its continental military traditions, the proximity of the Soviet Army, and the availability of powerful U.S. naval and tactical air forces. The U.S. investment in Europe's forward defense on the ground is, however, no less impressive, at least as a proportion of total U.S. ground forces. Despite potentially very demanding commitments in Korea and Southwest Asia, the bulk of U.S. ground forces remains dedicated to Europe's forward defense. Of the Army's 16 divisions, 10 are deployed in or slated for the rapid reinforcement of Europe; another five are considered to be available to NATO in extremis; only one—the 2nd Infantry Division, which is stationed in Korea—is not considered available for combat in Europe. Also earmarked for NATO are two of the Marine Corps' three Marine Amphibious Forces, each consisting of a division and an associated tactical air wing. In sum, out of a total of 19 active-duty U.S. ground force divisions, 17—or almost 90 percent—are dedicated in varying degrees to Europe's defense.

It also is to be noted that the U.S. Army's primary focus on Europe has dictated an historically disproportionate investment in comparatively expensive armored and mechanized infantry divisions; of the Army's 16 divisions, 12 are heavy. The real price of heaviness, however, has been severely degraded strategic mobility. Heavy forces represent a deliberate investment in firepower and tactical mobility at the expense of strategic mobility. Tanks and armored fighting vehicles can move rapidly on the battlefield, but their size and weight make it difficult to get them to the battlefield rapidly, especially if they are an ocean away.

Strategic mobility—the capacity to move military forces from one continent to another—is not a requirement for most European ground forces, which are stationed on the ground they are pledged to defend. This is not the case for most U.S. Army combat formations, whose operational availability in Europe, Southwest Asia, and the Far East can be assured only through enormous outlays for airlift, sealift, and, where possible, the prepositioning of additional sets of equipment in threatened areas. Thus the true cost of heavy U.S. ground forces includes the costs of those measures necessary to compensate for their inherent strategic immobility. A German, French, or Belgian tank division really costs but a fraction of a NATO-slated U.S. tank division stationed in the United States.

In sum, while in the broadest sense there has always been within NATO an understandable division of military labor based on the natural military strengths and weaknesses of its various members, there has also been a significant amount of what can be regarded from a purely military standpoint as unnecessary duplication of effort. This is especially true in the category of heavy ground forces committed to the forward defense of Germany, which in the case of U.S. ground forces impose inordinately heavy penalties in terms of money, strategic mobility, and, as will be seen, operational opportunity costs.

Unnecessary functional duplication is compounded by the emergent strategic indivisibility of Europe and Southwest Asia and the marked disparities in the ability and willingness of respective NATO members to project and maintain military power beyond the NATO Treaty area. As noted, the question of who should bear the burden of defending shared Western interests in Southwest Asia has generated rising controversy within the Alliance and has fueled congressional pressures on U.S. troop levels in Europe. Many U.S. senators and congressmen believe that Europe is not doing enough for its own defense or for the defense of Southwest Asia, upon whose oil Europe's economy is far more dependent than is that of the United States. Some are prepared to punish NATO allies by cutting the number of U.S. troops in Europe.

Attempts to resolve the issue of out-of-area burden-sharing must be predicated on recognition of certain military and political realities. The United States has long specialized in the kind of military forces best suited to handle all but the most demanding and unlikely contingencies in Southwest Asia and in other critical Third World regions where the West does not enjoy politically secure military access ashore. Within NATO the United States possesses a near monopoly or the lion's share of strategic airlift, militarily configured fast sealift, aerially refuelable tactical aircraft, fixed-wing carrier-based air power, and amphibious assault capabilities. With the exception of France, and to a lesser extent Great Britain, European members of NATO do not possess significant long-range airpower or sea-based force projection capabilities—the cutting edge of any effective intervention force in Southwest Asia.

Germany faces the most severe restraints on direct military participation in combat outside the Treaty area. Schooled for centuries in an operationally effective but strategically fatal continental military tradition, the German military continues to focus almost exclusively on the land battle in Central Europe. Germany lacks a sustained maritime tradition, a sizable navy, and any experience in transoceanic projection of power (Rommel's Afrika Korps, separated from Axis-controlled Europe by only 300 miles of water, ultimately having been defeated by the reassertion of Allied naval and air supremacy in the Central Mediterranean).

The employment of German armed forces outside the Treaty area is moreover shackled by political constraints. The Paris agreements of 1954, which paved the way for Germany's entry into NATO, limit active-duty German forces to 500,000 men, a ceiling at which the *Bundeswehr* is currently operating. As a matter of national policy, the *Bundeswehr* also is prohibited from engaging in combat outside the Treaty area, although this prohibition is vaguely worded and does not apply to peaceful deployments or to standing paramilitary forces like the *Bundesgrenzschutz* (Federal Border Guard), a unit of which successfully recaptured a hijacked Lufthansa airliner in Mogadishu in 1978. There do not appear to be any legal barriers to the peaceful exercising of *Bundeswehr* units beyond the Treaty area, and in fact two German warships were temporarily deployed to the Indian Ocean following the Soviet invasion of Afghanistan in 1979.

Even French and British out-of-area military capabilities are declining and are likely to continue to decline. The Falklands War of 1982 underscored the severely limited power projection capabilities of a Royal Navy that has been transformed into little more than an adjunct of NATO's antisubmarine warfare force; and the substantial cuts in France's conventional forces now being undertaken by the Mitterrand government, in favor of increased investment in nuclear deterrence, will fall disproportionately upon the French army and surface navy.

Most European members of NATO, however, continue to maintain small, strategically mobile, specialized ground force units—amphibious, airborne, mountain infantry, commando forces, and the like—that could, if provided sufficient lift and logistical support, play a significant role in Southwest Asian contingencies requiring such forces.

In short, Europe's military ability to participate directly in Southwest Asian contingencies is severely limited. Only the United States has at hand and can create sufficient amounts of the right kind of military power to embark upon the establishment of a credible deterrent to violent threats to common Western interests in Southwest Asia.

Any redeployment of significant allied active-duty forces from Europe to Southwest Asia would, moreover, weaken the defense of Europe itself. As noted, the defense of Europe is inseparable from the defense of Southwest Asia, and from the standpoint of military effectiveness it would be the height of folly to ignore the vastly differing operational requirements for the respective defense of the two regions (see discussion below). The United States logically specializes in the kind of military power most suited for contingencies in distant, logistically remote areas. In contrast, most European allies understandably have structured their forces primarily for the defense of their own territory against a threat whose character and magnitude are quite different from those confronting the West in Southwest Asia.

In combination, the growth of Europe's economic power and military potential in relation to that of the United States, the emergence of demanding new threats to shared Western interests in Southwest Asia, and the virtually singular ability of the United States to provide credible deterrence and defense in Southwest Asia—all suggest that what has until now been a rather crude and informal division of military labor within NATO should be made more deliberate, refined, and explicit.

The key features of a new division of military labor would be *a level of allied defense expenditure more commensurate with allied economic power, and eventual allied assumption of full responsibility for Europe's initial forward defense of the ground.* Eventual allied assumption of that responsibility would permit a substantial reduction in heavy U.S. ground forces now deployed in Germany and a reallocation of U.S. defense budgetary resources associated with the maintenance of those forces toward provision of expanded force projection, strategic mobility, and other specialized capabilities suitable for the defense of shared interests in Southwest Asia and elsewhere outside the NATO Treaty area. The United States, despite substantial real increases in defense expenditure, is not in a position to maintain the present magnitude of its commitment to Europe's forward defense while simultaneously creating an effective defense of distant Southwest Asia; only Europe, by devoting more resources to its own defense, can take up the strategic slack caused by the evolving character and locus of the Soviet military threat to the West.

Any proposed reduction in the U.S. military presence in Europe causes immediate official consternation on both sides of the Atlantic. What was in the late 1940s and early 1950s viewed (at least in Washington) as a temporary military shield designed to protect Europe's economic and military recovery from World War II soon came to be regarded, especially in Europe, as a more or less permanent and politically sensitive fixture of the international strategic cosmos. Europeans are wont to interpret any reduction in the U.S. military presence on the Continent, even for the most compelling strategic reasons, as tantamount to a weakening of America's basic commitment to their defense. The U.S. military is no less sensitive to proposed alterations in its force levels in Europe, since the present U.S. commitment to NATO, more than any other overseas obligation, drives the present size and structure of U.S. conventional forces, especially U.S. Army combat forces.

What is being proposed here is neither an abandonment of NATO nor a wholesale withdrawal of U.S. troops from Europe. A free and independent Western Europe is absolutely vital to the well-being of the United States. To be sure, the United States could survive the conquest of Western Europe by the Soviet Union. The price of survival, however, would be very high. The Soviet Union would gain control of the world's largest industrial plant; U.S. trade with Europe would virtually cease; democratic institutions in the United States itself would be forced to give way to those of a garrison state; and American culture would be denied a critical stimulus. Yet if America's defense is inseparable from Europe's defense, Europe's defense has become inseparable from the defense of Southwest Asia and other critical areas of the Third World.

What is proposed here is *a gradual and partial—albeit significant—reduction in U.S. heavy ground combat forces now deployed in Europe.* The U.S. Army Europe currently consists of five division equivalents: the 1st and 3rd Armored divisions, the 3rd and 8th Infantry (Mechanized) divisions, and three separate brigades. The withdrawal of three division equivalents would still leave behind the equivalent of an entire U.S. Army corps, assorted armored cavalry units, and the Berlin Brigade, which together with the retention in Europe of U.S. tactical air and theater nuclear forces now stationed there would leave in Europe a U.S. force presence of more than sufficient scope and distribution to guarantee the immediate and heavy engagement of U.S. combat units with Soviet forces in the event of war.

Allied ability to compensate for the loss of three U.S. heavy divisions is indisputable, especially if withdrawal of the divisions were conducted gradually over a period of, say, five or ten years. NATO Europe (including France) already provides 48 of the 53 U.S. and allied heavy divisions stationed in Europe and considered available for the defense of the Central Front. Moreover, the three new heavy divisions that NATO Europe would have to create need not all be active-duty formations, especially if their creation was accompanied by other measures aimed at improving Europe's forward conventional defense, such as the erection of barrier defenses along the inter-German border and a reconstitution of NATO's operational reserves.[5] European member states contributing to the defense of the Central Region collectively muster over 2,000,000 trained ground force reservists, and nations as disparate as the Netherlands, Sweden, Yugoslavia, and Israel have demonstrated that it is possible to maintain very ready reserve forces at little or no cost in combat skills and fighting power.

To be sure, Europe's assumption of greater responsibility for its initial forward defense on the ground would require increases in defense expenditure for the purchase of replacements for departing U.S. forces. These increases would be over and above those required to implement other conventional force improvements to which the Alliance committed itself in 1978 in the form of the Long-Term Defense Program (LTDP). Necessary budget increases would be modest, however, in comparison to those of the United States, which is currently sustaining annual real increases in defense spending averaging over eight percent from a baseline defense budget representing over six percent of its gross national product. In the judgment of Supreme Allied Commander Bernard W. Rogers, the goals of the LTDP can be realized with "an annual average real increase in [national] . . . defense spending of about four percent . . . for six years."[6] Those goals include designated improvements in readiness, reinforcement, reserve mobilization, maritime defense, air defense, command/control/communications, electronic warfare, logistics, and rationalization of armaments production. For perhaps just a fraction of another percentage point, NATO Europe could provide three additional heavy divisions along with their necessary combat support and logistics infrastructure.

Implicit in the proposed new functional and geographic division of labor is the demobilization of U.S. heavy forces returning from Europe, since a major aim of the new division of labor would be to permit a comparative reallocation of U.S. military resources away from Europe and toward provision of credible deterrence in Southwest Asia. Cutting the Army by three heavy divisions (and their respective "slices" of combat support and combat service support) would yield a reduction in authorized end-strength of approximately 135,000 personnel. A 13-division, 650,000-man Army would represent a savings of billions of dollars in annually recurring manpower, operating, and equipment costs, a savings which, if applied to enhancement of U.S. strategic mobility and force projection capabilities, could provide a major increase in the U.S. force presence outside the Treaty area.

For the U.S. Army, the implications of a new division of military labor within NATO are not confined to the issue of service end-strength. Europe's assumption of primary responsibility for its ground defense, coupled with the urgent need for forces rapidly deployable to Southwest Asia, argues strongly for increased emphasis on light, strategically mobile forces tailored to meet the unusual natural and operational demands of combat in that region. Those demands place a premium on special operations, mountain warfare, airborne, airmobile, and light armored forces. New technologies, force structures, and tactical doctrines of the kind now being explored and tested by the Army's 9th Division, if properly integrated, offer the prospect of generating significant levels of firepower and tactical mobility without paying traditional penalties in strategic mobility. Properly configured light forces also could play a major role in exploiting the Soviet military's excessively rigid and centralized command and control system in a conflict in Europe (see Chapter 8). In short, implicit in the proposed new division of military labor is a smaller, lighter, more agile U.S. Army emphasizing specialized rather than general purpose forces. The U.S. Army's principal role would be one often envisaged since the Korean War but never realized: a central mobile ground force reserve dedicated to the defense of U.S. and allied interests in circumstances where local forces alone are unable to deal effectively with the threat.

To enhance the U.S. capacity to defend shared Western interests in Southwest Asia, the additional defense resources afforded by a smaller U.S. Army should be applied in three critical areas: strategic mobility, forcible-entry capabilities, and sea-based air power and logistical support. For the United States, the pivotal conditions governing any successful military intervention in Southwest Asia are distance and the lack of politically secure military access ashore in peacetime. No area of the world is more distant from the United States than the Persian Gulf. Air distances from the U.S. eastern coast exceed 7,000 nautical miles; by sea, over which most of the present Rapid Deployment Force would be compelled to move, distances range from 8,500 nautical miles via the Suez Canal to 12,000 nautical miles via the Cape of Good Hope.

The logistical significance of these distances is a function of three factors. First, most of the ground and tactical air forces currently earmarked for the Rapid Deployment Force (RDF) that was established in 1980 to protect U.S. interests in the Persian Gulf are stationed in the United States, requiring an enormous investment in means of moving them quickly to the Gulf area. Second, with the exception of tiny Diego Garcia, the United States possesses no military bases in the Southwest Asian region, imposing unusually demanding requirements for provisioning the RDF once it is deployed to the Gulf. Third, Soviet and other potentially hostile forces immediately available for combat in the region are larger and much closer to the Gulf, condemning at least early-arriving RDF forces to an almost certain and pronounced numerical inferiority.

The adverse operational consequences of the Gulf's logistical remoteness would be exacerbated in contingencies requiring commitment of substantial U.S. ground forces ashore. Surface naval and amphibious forces can be maintained on station indefinitely in the region. Land-based tactical air forces can be moved quickly from the United States to the Gulf if, of course, provided access to air installations en route and in the Gulf itself. Sizable ground forces, however, especially heavy Army formations, cannot be moved quickly by air or by sea.

Current Defense Department programs to enhance the RDJTF's strategic mobility, which include procurement of 50 additional C-5 strategic air transport planes, 44 KC-10 cargo-tanker aircraft, eight fast deployment logistics ships, and 13 specially configured maritime prepositioning ships designed to serve as floating warehouses of equipment in the Indian Ocean, will not eliminate the large gap that now exists between forces assigned to the RDJTF and the ability to move them rapidly overseas. Nor do the mobility enhancement programs offer a solution to the threat of preemption by, for example, Soviet airborne forces (or other potentially hostile forces close to the point of dispute), whose strategic mobility is calculable in hours and days rather than weeks or months.

The deterrent value of a preemptive deployment of Soviet airborne forces in a U.S.–Soviet confrontation in the Gulf should not be underestimated. Indeed, it has been persuasively argued that success in such a confrontation would crown not the side that got to the contested ground in larger force but the side that simply got there first with any measurable force:

> The United States does not have ground forces stationed on the territory that would be threatened, and geography favors the Soviets in a countdown toward competitive intervention. *The Middle East is an area in which preemption is the only reasonable strategy for either of the superpowers*; preemption not in terms of strikes against each other's forces, but in terms of reaching the scene first. Once one of the superpowers' troops are on the disputed ground, counterintervention becomes a much more reckless venture for the other, because he then has the "last clear chance" to avoid the dangers inherent in undertaking the unprecedented action of combat between two nuclear-armed states. The danger of surprise here, for the United States, is not so much the edge it can give as a force multiplier in determining the outcome of battle; rather it is the danger that by being slow on the draw, Washington may be deterred from any direct engagement at all.[7]

It should go without saying that a strategy of preemption is ill-served by an intervention force based largely in distant North America and lacking the strategic mobility necessary to ensure timely arrival in the Gulf of more than token ground forces. Nor is such a strategy served by the RDF's current concept of operations, which focuses heavily on a "worst-case" scenario involving a massive, albeit leisurely, Soviet invasion of Iran preceded by warning time ample enough to permit deployment to the Gulf of the bulk of U.S. Army forces assigned to the RDJTF. A full-blooded Soviet invasion of Iran, while undoubtedly the most demanding contingency for the RDF in Southwest Asia, is also the least likely to materialize of all the potential threats to shared Western interests, which include intrastate upheavals of the kind that toppled the Shah of Iran and regional interstate wars like that being played out between Iraq and Iran.

A successful U.S. defense of Iran against a Soviet attack may not be feasible in any event, given the assumptions on which it is predicated. Those assumptions include: (1) early U.S. access to Turkish air bases for the purpose of conducting an interdiction campaign against Soviet forces pouring into northwestern Iran; (2) access to Saudi and other local military facilities for the purpose of staging a defense of southern Iran; (3) Iranian acquiescence to the presence of U.S. forces on its territory; (4) the ability and willingness of the U.S. Navy to keep the Straits of Hormuz open against threats posed by Soviet Backfire bombers and attack submarines; and (5) Soviet willingness to confine the conflict to Southwest Asia.[8]

Compounding the penalties imposed by distance is the lack of politically secure military access ashore in Southwest Asia in peacetime. Southwest Asia is not Europe or Northeast Asia, where the United States maintains powerful forces ashore amidst reliable and militarily competent allies.

The projection of U.S. military power into logistically remote areas overseas has always required a network of secure refueling, resupply, and maintenance facilities on the fringes of the disputed region—a logistical network that, without exception, has been based on land. No such infrastructure exists today in Southwest Asia. As noted by the RDF's first commander:

There are sizable U.S. forces in-place in Western Europe—with the exception of naval forces in the Indian Ocean, we have none in Southwest Asia.

There are sizable amounts of prepositioned supplies and equipment in Western Europe for reinforcing units—we have none in Southwest Asia.

There is an in-place command and control system in Western Europe—we have none in Southwest Asia.

There is an extensive in-place logistics infrastructure in Western Europe—we have none in Southwest Asia.

There are extensive host-nation support agreements between the U.S. and Western Europe countries—we have none in Southwest Asia.

There is an alliance of military allies in Western Europe—there is no such alliance in Southwest Asia.[9]

Except for Diego Garcia, some 2,500 miles from the Strait of Hormuz, the United States possesses no military bases in that vast area of the world stretching from Turkey to the Philippines. Nor are prospects favorable for establishing a major facility in the region. The countries in the area most emphatically do not want formal security arrangements with the United States.

The political sensitivity of potential host nations to a permanent U.S. military presence on their own soil is understandable. Such a presence would validate the criticisms of radical Arabs about how the conservative Gulf states are lackeys of the United States, thus undermining the internal legitimacy of the very regimes the United States seeks to protect. A U.S. force presence ashore is probably undesirable in any event, since, as illustrated by the truck-bomb assault on U.S. Marine headquarters in Beirut on October 23, 1983, it almost certainly would attract radical terrorist or guerrilla attacks. (Lest it be forgotten, the first U.S. ground combat units deployed to Vietnam were sent there not to defend the South Vietnamese but to defend U.S. air installations in that country.)

To be sure, the Defense Department has not been insensitive to the political barriers to establishing a permanent military presence ashore in the Gulf region, and has sought with some success to gain contingent rights of access to selected facilities in Kenya, Somalia, Oman, and Egypt. Yet simply having the promise of access to facilities on a contingency basis is no substitute for U.S.-controlled and -operated bases whose use is not subject to momentary political calculations of host governments in a crisis. The same internal political considerations that deny the United States a permanent military presence ashore in the region in peacetime could well be invoked to deny the United States access to facilities in the event of crisis. During the October War of 1973 the United States was denied overflight rights by NATO allies, countries usually regarded as more reliable than nontreaty U.S. "friends" in the Gulf.

The problems of distance and access, as well as the persuasive case for adopting a strategy of preemptive deployment, ought to have propelled the Pentagon toward creation of an intervention force quite different from the present RDF. Instead of a large, distant, logistically ponderous, Vietnam-style intervention force dependent on friendly invitation to go ashore and stay there, logic and common sense would seem to dictate a small, agile, tactically capable force that is based at sea, supplied from the sea, and supported by expanded sea power, especially carrier-based aviation and forcible-entry capabilities. Such a force would stress quality, not size; on-station presence and immediate responsiveness, not tardy arrivals from the United States; and logistical self-sufficiency, not dependence on facilities ashore.[10]

The lack of any real prospect for establishing an operationally significant peacetime U.S. military presence ashore in southwest Asia (to say nothing of its questionable desirability) compels a primary reliance on sea power, especially survivable sea-based air power and the kind of sea-based capability to project power ashore long embodied in the Navy-Fleet Marine Force team. The refusal of potential host nations to permit the United States to position significant military forces or materiel on their territory also argues strongly for expanding current plans to position both aboard specialized ships to be maintained in the Indian Ocean. The inherent mobility and security of ships at sea additionally provide greater military flexibility in a crisis and greater security against terrorist and guerrilla attacks.

A sea-based RDF admittedly would have limited utility in contingencies demanding sustained inland combat in and beyond the reach of amphibious assault forces and carrier-based air power. However, prosecution of sustained inland combat, which would be carried out by new, light, specially tailored U.S. Army forces and, if necessary, heavy ground units based in the United States, would be contingent upon securing coastal lodgments, which can be gained only by the ability to land U.S. forces. Moreover, unlike forces held in reserve in the United States for rapid deployment to Southwest Asia, a sea-based RDF could be maintained on the spot, providing a level of deterrence and a capacity for preemptive insertion unattainable by forces stationed in the United States.

To conclude that the United States militarily must bear the brunt of defending Southwest Asia is not to conclude that the United States can or should go it alone, or that European allies cannot provide substantial indirect assistance. A more rational division of military labor within NATO along the lines suggested cannot disregard certain political realities. A Southwest Asian contingency in which only Americans got killed in defense of continued access to Persian Gulf oil, upon which Europe is far more dependent than North America, could provoke a public and congressional reaction politically catastrophic to the Alliance. The Stevens Amendment of 1982, which called for a punitive unilateral reduction in U.S. troop strength in Europe by some 23,000 men, was motivated in large measure by anger at European allies perceived to be unwilling to bear their fair share of the common defense burden both in Europe and in Southwest Asia. Although the amendment failed to secure passage, it is likely to be resubmitted in the future.

In the event of a major conflict in Southwest Asia, it is politically imperative that at least token allied forces be present in the battle area. In the meantime, it is no less imperative that allies be willing—and be seen to be willing—to render the United States all possible forms of indirect assistance in planning for Southwest Asian contingencies.

With respect to direct allied participation, many European allies, as noted, already possess strategically mobile specialized ground force units suitable for many possible contingencies. If provided sufficient logistical support and strategic lift by the United States, those forces could be brought to bear in a Southwest Asian crisis. As former colonial powers, several European allies also possess extensive knowledge of the political and operational environments of Southwest Asia and other critical Third World areas—knowledge that could mean the difference between successful and unsuccessful military intervention.

The major obstacle to allied out-of-area deployment is, of course, the political reluctance of most allied governments to commit any forces outside the Treaty area. Some allies do not regard the threats to Western interests in Southwest Asia as serious; others take them seriously but question the utility of military responses; still others conclude that Southwest Asia is an exclusively U.S. responsibility, and that the United States can be counted upon to fulfill that responsibility irrespective of what the rest of the Alliance does. Few seem to appreciate the potentially fatal danger to Alliance political cohesion inherent in an exclusively American force presence in Southwest Asia. If it is politically vital to Europeans that Americans be among the first day's casualties in a war in Europe, it is no less politically vital to Americans that at least a few Europeans be among the first in a Southwest Asian conflict. As *The Economist* has trenchantly observed,

> . . . the question is whether Europe will take up some of the burden in the Gulf, or whether it will continue to do nothing until the American defense budget comes under such pressure that the Americans blow the lid off NATO by withdrawing a large number of their troops from Europe in order to save money for the RDF.[11]

Many Europeans dwell on the fact that the North Atlantic Treaty Organization is dedicated exclusively to the defense of Europe and that the mutual member-state defense obligations under the NATO Treaty apply only to a specific region of the world. This is true, but it ignores the reality that events in Southwest Asia can be just as detrimental to European security as events along the inter-German border. Some also seem to have forgotten that the Treaty has not barred individual member-states from taking unilateral or even joint military action outside the Treaty area since 1949, as did several in Korea, the Dutch in Indonesia, the French and British in Egypt, the French in Algeria, the British in East Africa, the Belgians in the Congo (Zaire), the United States in Indochina, and the Portuguese in Angola and Mozambique. In few of these cases were vital common Western interests as threatened as they are today in Southwest Asia.

NATO is admittedly an organization ill-suited for the promotion of an integrated, common Western military response to threats beyond the Treaty area. What is needed is an informal coalition of the willing and able that is prepared to deal with military challenges outside the Treaty area on an ad hoc, contingency-by-contingency basis in a manner similar to that which led to the U.S. provision of critical strategic airlift assets in support of French intervention in Shaba province in 1978. For such a coalition to be militarily effective, there should be established an informal military working group that would entail exchanges of intelligence information and joint planning.

The possibility of conducting joint military exercises outside the Treaty area with units assigned to the RDF also should be explored.

With respect to indirect forms of allied assistance to the United States in mounting and maintaining a credible defense of common Western interests in Southwest Asia, it is imperative that the United States be assured of certain overflight and transit rights over and on allied territory. As noted, almost all of the ground and tactical air units assigned to the Rapid Deployment Force are based in the United States. Thus for the present RDF to be effective, it must have unimpeded lines of communication to the Persian Gulf during a crisis. The same would be true even for a sea-based RDF, which although initially logistically self-sufficient, would, in a large or protracted contingency, be no less dependent on resupply and reinforcement from the United States. A repeat of the allies' performance during the October War of 1973 could endanger timely military intervention; it would certainly spur more congressional calls for punitive unilateral U.S. troop withdrawals from Europe.

Second, the richer European allies (and Japan) can and should help the United States finance the numerous RDF-related military construction projects in the Southwest Asian region. Completion of these projects is essential to the logistical sustainability of the RDF as it is now configured and would be essential in contingencies exceeding the resources of a sea-based RDF. Partial allied financing of these projects would be very welcome in the Congress and ought to be a "natural" for Germany, already heavily involved in supporting the U.S. military infrastructure on its own territory and hobbled by singular restraints on the deployment of its own forces outside the NATO Treaty area.

A third form of indirect allied assistance would be the provision of specialized merchant vessels on a lease-back basis and the outright purchase, for joint use, of U.S. strategic transport aircraft. Many European allies possess merchant fleets much larger than our own and containing significant numbers of modern, militarily useful vessels, like roll-on/roll-off ships. Despite the efforts of the Reagan Administration, the RDF continues to suffer a major shortfall in fast sealift as well as sealift capable of rapidly loading and unloading bulky military cargoes. An allied commitment to lease even a dozen of the right vessels to the U.S. Military Sealift Command would go a long way down the road to eliminating this shortfall.

With regard to strategic airlift, as has been noted, the RDF will face a no less substantial shortfall even upon completion of the Reagan Administration's current strategic airlift programs. No European ally, including the French with their far-flung African commitments, possesses military transport aircraft comparable to the C-5, C-141, or KC-10. Given the longstanding critical shortage in strategic airlift dedicated to the U.S. reinforcement of Europe itself, and the continuing availability of C-5s and KC-10s, U.S. allies, individually or in a consortium, can and ought to relieve the United States of bearing the sole burden within the Alliance of providing the strategic airlift needed to defend both Europe and

Southwest Asia. If undertaken under a proper shared-use arrangement, allied purchase of, say, two dozen C-5s and KC-10s would make that many more available for U.S. or joint U.S.–allied use in either theater of operations.

A fourth form of indirect allied assistance would be the provision of a token standing naval force presence in the Indian Ocean. Such a presence need not entail more than a half-dozen ships—say, one each from the German, Dutch, British, Italian, Spanish, and Portuguese navies (the French naval presence in the Indian Ocean is already large)—and could be maintained at little cost to Western naval capabilities dedicated to the defense of the NATO Treaty area. Though militarily insignificant, such a force, especially if it engaged in joint exercises with French and U.S. naval forces routinely maintained in the region, could blunt congressional irritation with Europe on a very intense issue as well as underscore shared Western concern over the fate of Southwest Asia.

Realization of the new division of military labor within NATO proposed here ultimately hinges on the political willingness of NATO Europe to embrace levels of defense expenditure more commensurate with its economic power. In this regard there is little ground for optimism, at least in the near term. Most allied governments are beset by serious economic problems and preside over entrenched welfare states and political cultures posing formidable obstacles to sustained real increases in national defense spending on the order of four percent, as proposed by General Rogers. Few have consistently complied even with the three percent goal to which all armed members of the Alliance pledged themselves in 1978, despite a worsening conventional force balance in Europe and mounting threats to Western access to Persian Gulf oil. Indeed, a Pentagon report released in June 1983 concluded that allied defense expenditure for 1983 would average but one percent in real terms over that of 1982.[12]

The author does not presume to have discovered a means of convincing Europe to do more for its own defense. Even the most forceful and inspired American leadership might not be able to do so. As long as allies continue to accept the facts of nuclear stalemate and the evolving locus and character of Soviet threats to shared interests but refuse to act upon their obvious implications, a credible defense of those interests will continue to elude the West, whether or not that defense entails a new division of military labor.

The rub is that a continuation of military business as usual on the part of NATO Europe could well provoke a public and congressional reaction in the United States that, in the end, could destroy the Alliance itself. It is perhaps again pertinent to recall that deployment of large U.S. ground forces to Europe in the early 1950s was predicated on the assumption that Europe's eventual economic recovery would make such a presence no longer necessary. As President Eisenhower himself observed, in the closing months of his second Administration, "For eight years I believed that a reduction of American strength in Europe should be initiated as soon as the European economies were restored. I believe that time has come."[13] The case for a new transatlantic military relationship is even stronger today.

Pulling [U.S.] troops out of Western Europe would not be turning our back on the West Europeans as critics argue. Rather it would indicate that the U.S. is seeking a redefined transatlantic partnership where the balance would be restored between each partner's economic and political status on the one hand, and its military contributions on the other. In the short run, this undoubtedly would involve some harsh trade-offs within Western Europe between welfare state goods and military expenditures. But in the longer view, the trade-offs would be worth it, because it would put Western Europe on an equal footing with the U.S. in defending the Western values and institutions both subscribe to.

And while it may be true that the West Europeans may not be willing to give up some part of their welfare states to defend themselves, in which case a U.S. troop pullout could lead to further accommodation of the Soviets by Western Europe, it is better we know this sooner than later.[14]

Critics undoubtedly will condemn the author's proposed new division of military labor within the Atlantic Alliance as simply another call for America's reversion to a "maritime strategy," regarded by some as little more than an intellectual cloak for a return to the old-time strategic religion of military isolationism, unilateralism, and Fortress America. Nothing could be further from the truth. Indeed, the current debate between so-called maritime and coalition (or continental) warfare strategists[15] is somewhat misleading. To the author's knowledge, no "maritime strategist" has argued that the U.S. possesses no security interests overseas worth defending or proposed that U.S. allies on the Eurasian landmass ought to be left to fend for themselves; nor have even the most devout of "coalition strategists" denied that a successful defense of U.S. military commitments overseas hinges in the first instance upon the ability to control the seas linking the United States to those commitments. The real issues are (1) the relative emphasis, within a framework of invariably finite resources, to be accorded to sea power versus ground and tactical air power; and (2) the most effective means of securing control of the seas in the event of war. Robust sea power is essential to the prosecution of coalition warfare, but sea power itself is no substitute for forward-deployed ground and tactical air forces.

It should, moreover, be apparent by now that the author regards, as has every U.S. administration since 1950, coalition warfare as the foundation of any credible U.S. military strategy, and that the proposed new division of military labor within the Atlantic Alliance is designed to strengthen the effectiveness of coalition warfare. It does not entertain abandonment, formal or informal, of any U.S. treaty or other ally, but rather militarily modest, albeit politically difficult alterations in current U.S. and NATO conventional force posture.

NOTES

1. For a superb exposition on the subject, see Richard K. Betts, *Suprise Attack, Lessons for Defense Planning* (Washington, D.C.: The Brookings Institution, 1982).

2. Ulrich de Maiziere, "How Can Germany Best Be Defended?" *AEI Foreign Policy and Defense Review*, 4:3/4 (March, 1983), 9.
3. Iceland has no military forces, and tiny Luxembourg maintains but 690 men under arms.
4. According to the London-based International Institute for Strategic Studies, the Soviet Army contains 46 tank divisions, 119 mechanized infantry divisions, 8 airborne divisions, and 14 artillery divisions.
5. See the author's "Forward Defense and Striking Deep," *Armed Forces Journal* (November, 1983).
6. General Bernard W. Rogers, "The Atlantic Alliance: Prescriptions for a Difficult Decade," *Foreign Affairs* (Summer, 1982), p. 1155.
7. Betts, *Surprise Attack*, p. 262.
8. See the author's "The RDF: Is the Pentagon Kidding?" *The Washington Quarterly* (Summer, 1981).
9. Statement by Lieutenant General P. X. Kelley before the Senate Armed Services Subcommittee on Sea Power and Force Projection, March 9, 1981, p. 5.
10. For a discussion of an effective sea-based logistics system, see the author's *The Rapid Deployment Force and U.S. Military Intervention in the Persian Gulf*, pp. 78–81.
11. "Will Europe Help America Help Europe?" *The Economist* (December 11, 1982), p. 64.
12. "Pentagon Report to Congress Hits NATO Allies' Defense Spending," *Washington Post* (June 29, 1983), p. 21.
13. Dwight D. Eisenhower, quoted in *Congressional Record* (August 11, 1952), p. 5714.
14. Melvyn B. Krauss, "It's Time to Change the Atlantic Alliance," *Wall Street Journal* (March 3, 1983), p. 24.
15. See, for example, Robert W. Komer, "Maritime Strategy vs. Coalition Defense," *Foreign Affairs* (Summer, 1982), pp. 1124-1143; and Stansfield Turner and George Thibault, "Preparing for the Unexpected: The Need for a New Military Strategy," *Foreign Affairs* (Fall, 1982), pp. 122–135.

CHAPTER 7.
A CLOSER STRATEGIC ENGAGEMENT OF CHINA

As noted earlier, China constitutes an irreplaceable strategic counterweight to the Soviet Union, tying down large Soviet ground, naval, and tactical air forces that might otherwise be deployed opposite Europe and Southwest Asia. Without this counterweight there would be no possibility of developing a new U.S. military strategy based on a reasonable harmonization of ends and means.

The issue addressed here is whether the common interest of China and the United States in containing Soviet "hegemonism" on the Eurasian landmass can and ought to be translated into more active channels of military communication and cooperation than exist today. This is a knotty question whose answer is unavoidably shaped by judgments of China's current and anticipated military strengths and weaknesses, and by highly speculative assumptions about China's future leadership and her likely behavior in future crises or wars that in one degree or another involved China's security interests. There is, too, the question of whether a close, sustained strategic relationship between two so fundamentally antithetical societies is possible, and, if so, the effects of such a relationship on long-term U.S.–Soviet relations.

It is here assumed that nothing short of a Soviet attack on China itself could induce China to participate directly in a war against the Soviet Union. China's conventional military forces lack the ability to sustain significant offensive operations on Soviet territory; indeed, for the foreseeable future the People's Liberation Army (PLA) will lack the ability even to mount an effective forward defense of Sinkiang, Inner Mongolia, and Manchuria against a determined Soviet attack. The comparatively ill-trained and poorly equipped hordes of the PLA are simply no match for the Soviets' modern and fully mechanized ground forces and technologically advanced frontal aviation. Only in circumstances involving a Soviet attempt to conquer and occupy China's densely populated areas far to the south of its relatively barren border provinces might the PLA, by reverting to tried and true methods of "people's war," be able to achieve a stand-off and impose upon the Soviet Union costs eventually exceeding gains. Such a scenario, however, presumes unimaginable stupidity on the part of the Kremlin.

To be sure, equipping the PLA with modern weapons comparable to those they confront in Soviet forces along the border would improve its capabilities, although it would not afford the PLA the capacity for offensive operations against the Soviet Union itself that could favorably affect the outcome of a war in Europe.

It should be noted that the PLA has relatively little experience in modern warfare, a deficiency that was glaringly evident in its tactically dismal performance against seasoned and well-equipped North Vietnamese regulars during China's punitive incursion into Vietnam in 1979. China, moreover, lacks the necessary educational base and technical and logistical infrastructure to support a large, modern military establishment.

There is also the question of cost. An estimated 200–400 billion dollars would be required to modernize the entire PLA[1] by simply purchasing outright the necessary weapons and equipment. This is a sum impossible to extract from an economy with an estimated gross national product of less than $500 billion; and in any event no single country or group of potential foreign suppliers could possibly produce the weapons and equipment required in less than a decade. It is for this reason that China has pursued an alternative approach of modest purchases of selected military equipment and technologies with the aim of eventually reproducing them at home.

This is not to suggest that more cannot be done in the way of enhancing China's near-term defenses against a potential Soviet attack. Former Secretary of Defense Harold Brown has concluded that

> . . . a substantial improvement toward a more modest goal—improving the PRC's capability to defend itself against armored and air attack—could be made through the development or procurement of more modern antitank and antiaircraft systems. Here an investment of $10 billion over six or seven years—less than 10 percent of present PRC defense costs—would make an enormous difference.[2]

Since a China capable of defending itself against the Soviet Union is in the strategic interest of the United States, and since at least in the near term it would be cheaper for China to procure selected defensive weapons abroad than to develop them on her own, the United States should be prepared to sell such weapons to Beijing and to encourage NATO allies to do likewise. The object would be to increase the potential costs to the Soviets of even a limited attack on China's northern provinces by providing Beijing comparatively cheap but effective defensive technologies. Such technologies might include wire-guided antiarmor missiles, short-range surface-to-air missiles, air defense radars, communications equipment, electronic countermeasures devices, and transport aircraft and helicopters.

Yet even a China capable of offering an effective forward defense of provinces most exposed to a Soviet attack would still be incapable of initiating a second front against the Soviets in the Far East in the event of a global conflict that began in Europe. The ability to sustain major offensive operations deep in Soviet territory will be denied to China for the foreseeable future. To put it another way, China's value as a strategic counterweight to the Soviet Union in the event of war will continue to hinge upon perceptions and decisions in Moscow, not Beijing. Western arms transfers to China can strengthen China's ability to resist a Soviet attack, but they cannot endow Beijing the capacity to hold Soviet forces in the Far East hostage to the threat of a Chinese attack against the Soviet Union. "China," concludes Allen S. Whiting, "lacks virtually all of the factors necessary to play the role of swing-weight between the two superpowers during the coming decade."[3]

China's puny ability to help the West in the event of war with the Soviet Union changes dramatically, however, with respect to regional conflicts involving other challenges to shared Sino-American strategic interests in Asia. And it is here that the foundation for a more active Sino-American military relationship can and ought to be laid. The most obvious non-Soviet threat to shared interests in Asia is the prospect of Vietnamese military expansion beyond Indochina. Both China and the United States regard Vietnam as a surrogate for Soviet expansionism in Asia; both have an important interest in the preservation of Thailand; and both have at one time or another gone to war against Hanoi.

It is difficult to conceive of a more powerful deterrent to a Vietnamese invasion of Thailand than the threat of *concerted* action by Chinese ground forces and American naval and airpower. Yet, to be effective, such a deterrent would have to be based not only on a Sino-American declaration that both countries would oppose an attempted Vietnamese conquest of Thailand, but also on the establishment in advance, via joint military staff discussions, of joint contingency plans designed to coordinate the employment of Chinese ground forces and U.S. naval and tactical air forces. Such plans conceivably could encompass a U.S. naval blockade of major Vietnamese ports; a U.S. air interdiction campaign against Vietnamese supply lines in Laos and Cambodia; U.S. provision of selected advanced weaponry to the PLA; China's establishment of a second front through an advance into Vietnam's northeastern provinces bordering on China (à la the Chinese incursion of 1979); and Chinese provision of temporary U.S. access to naval and air bases on Hainan Island and the Luichow Peninsula for the purposes of surveillance, blockade, and interdiction.

Although preparation for military collaboration would in the near term be confined to deterrence of further Vietnamese aggression in Southeast Asia, it could provide the basis for a more active collaboration against other threats to shared interests in Asia on a case-by-case basis. For example, both China and the United States have an important shared interest in supporting Afghanistan's resistance to Soviet occupation; Soviet forces tied down in Afghanistan are forces unavailable for deployment opposite Europe or Sinkiang or Manchuria. China is believed to be supplying weapons to the Afghani resistance. China also is much closer to that country, whereas U.S. access to Afghanistan is limited both by distance and by Pakistani political sensitivities. Yet China cannot provide the Afghanis the kind of small, effective antiarmor and antihelicopter weapons they so desperately need and which the United States manufactures in comparative abundance. Does not all of this suggest a promising avenue of Sino-American military cooperation?

Beyond prospects for Sino-American military collaboration in Southeast Asia and Afghanistan there looms the ultimate potential expression of a military "entente cordial": U.S. assistance to Beijing in the event of a Soviet attack on China itself. To be sure, the United States is already militarily overextended, and is not now or ever likely to be in a military position to affect decisively the outcome of a full-scale war between China and the Soviet Union. U.S. ground forces would be virtually irrelevant in such a conflict, and U.S. naval and tactical air power could not make anything more than a marginal contribution without uncovering vital U.S. interests in Europe and Southwest Asia. Direct U.S. participation in China's defense would in any event risk war with the Soviet Union. On the other hand, a United States prepared to supply China defensive weapons and technologies in peacetime should also be prepared to supply them in wartime. To repeat, it is in the strategic interest of both Beijing and Washington to deter a Soviet attack on China, and in the event that deterrence fails, to make an attack as costly as possible.

In sum, prospects for a closer strategic engagement of China in the longer term are promising, if not directly against the Soviet Union then against other threats to shared vital interests in the region. The United States should pursue these prospects vigorously and irrespective of continuing differences with China over such other issues as bilateral trade, the future of Taiwan, and the presence of U.S. forces in Korea. At the very least, the United States should not permit those differences to fester to the point where some in Beijing might be encouraged to explore the possibility of a rapprochement with Moscow. Former President Richard M. Nixon has warned, "It would be the height of folly to try to 'save' Taiwan at the cost of losing China. If China slipped back into the Soviet orbit, the balance of power in the world would be shifted overwhelmingly against us."[4]

This is not to suggest that the United States should abandon Taiwan to Beijing's tender mercies or capitulate to China's wishes on other matters in contention. Ultimately it is for China to decide whether an independent Taiwan poses a greater danger to her security than the Russian Bear sitting along her northern borders.

NOTES

1. Harold Brown, *Thinking About National Security, Defense and Foreign Policy in a Dangerous World* (Boulder, Colo.: Westview Press, 1983), p. 127.
2. Ibid. pp. 127–128.
3. Allen S. Whiting, "Sino-American Relations: The Decade Ahead," *Orbis* (Fall 1982), p. 701.
4. Richard M. Nixon, quoted in *New York Times* (February 28, 1982).

CHAPTER 8.
EXPLOITING SOVIET WEAKNESSES

The third element of any new strategy designed to bring U.S. and allied military power and obligations into closer alignment would be a declaratory war-fighting doctrine dedicated to a more deliberate exploitation of specific Soviet military weaknesses. All military establishments have inherent strengths and weaknesses, and applying one's own strengths against an enemy's weaknesses—while seeking to prevent the enemy from doing the same—has been a fundamental principle of successful operational planning and execution since the days of Alexander the Great.

For the United States and its allies, however, it is not just a principle but an imperative. Given the Soviet Union's enormous geographic advantages with respect to potential conflict on or along much of the Eurasian landmass, and her possession of numerically superior ground and tactical air forces opposite Europe and Southwest Asia, any opposing strategy designed to slug it out with Soviet forces man for man, tank for tank, and plane for plane is a recipe for probable defeat. A head-on attempt to grind down Soviet forces ignores the reality that attrition warfare is a viable option only for the resource-superior side (i.e., the side capable of both inflicting and sustaining larger losses over a longer period of time). Attrition warfare worked for the United States in World War I and World War II because powerful allies succeeded in denying conclusive victory to the operationally superior field forces of resource-inferior Germany long enough to permit the United States to mobilize its vast military potential and bring it to bear with ultimately decisive results.

Yet in a future conflict that lasted no more than six months or even a year, it is the Warsaw Pact and not NATO that would enjoy resource superiority in terms of standing and mobilizable forces that could be employed in combat. Only in a protracted war could NATO eventually mobilize power commensurate with its vastly greater economic power, and thereby confront the Warsaw Pact with decisive defeat. It is in part for this reason that the Soviet Union, like the Third Reich before it, has adopted a military posture based upon the maintenance in peacetime of disproportionately large standing and readily mobilizable forces that are structured, in the event of war and regardless of the circumstances attending the outbreak of hostilities, for an immediate assumption of rapid offensive operations designed to defeat NATO before the Alliance could fully mobilize its ultimately superior military potential. And it is for this reason that the Soviets, if denied a decisive victory early on, would be sorely tempted to resort to nuclear fire as an alternative to a protracted non-nuclear conflict.

In a war, time would be on the side of NATO, not the Warsaw Pact. The issue for the Alliance has always been whether its smaller standing forces in Central Europe could hold on long enough, without resort to nuclear weapons, to buy the time needed to translate its superior military potential into decisive results on the battlefield. The outlook is not promising. As General David C. Jones, former Chairman of the Joint Chiefs of Staff, has observed:

> In the past, we had time to overcome our mistakes. Our allies often bore the initial brunt, and we had the industrial capacity for a quick buildup in the military capacity needed to turn the tide. Today we can expect no such respite. Our allies could not delay the Soviet Union while we prepared, and our industrial base has fallen into a state of disrepair. Nuclear weapons have added new dimensions which make constant readiness even more critical. If we are to deter another conflict, or to succeed if one be thrust upon us, we must be prepared to do things right on the battlefield the first time.[1]

The issue is not, as it has so often and erroneously been defined, whether NATO should plan to fight a short war or a long war, but whether the Alliance can muster a successful forward defense of Germany in the first few weeks of combat against numerically superior Warsaw Pact forces possessing the inestimable advantages associated with the initiation of hostilities.

None of this is to suggest that the Soviets could be defeated without heavy losses on both sides. Certainly in Central Europe head-on attrition battles would be unavoidable, especially given NATO Center's lack of depth and the Alliance's commitment to forward defense, although the Alliance's present concept of forward defense leaves much to be desired. Attrition alone, however, offers no prospect of a successful defense; it must be supplemented by other approaches.

As a substitute for the impossible mission of attempting to defeat a Soviet attack solely through attrition, which, even if it succeeded, would entail a level of destruction in NATO Europe unacceptable to many allies, the Alliance must adopt a war-fighting doctrine designed to offset the Warsaw Pact's quantitative preponderance through the application of specific Alliance military strengths against specific Soviet weaknesses. As the numerically inferior side in terms of standing forces, NATO must, like Germany in the late 1930s and early 1940s and Israel for the past three decades, substitute brains for brawn and quality for quantity on the battlefield.

Despite its large standing forces and central position on the Eurasian landmass, the Soviet Union possesses a number of military weaknesses. What follows is a discussion of those weaknesses and suggested means of taking advantage of them.

UNRELIABLE ALLIES

It has been said that the Soviet Union is the only nation in the world surrounded by hostile communist countries. While perhaps an overstatement, the Soviet Union, unlike the United States, does not enjoy politically reliable military partners. The Warsaw Pact is, after all, an alliance of enforced rather than voluntary loyalty. With the exceptions of Bulgaria and East Germany, none of the Soviet Union's East European allies could be counted upon to provide assured political and military support for a Soviet offensive against Western Europe. Yet to sustain the momentum of a drive against NATO, the Soviets would be compelled to move massive reinforcements and supplies from western Russia across Eastern Europe, including Poland, Czechoslovakia, and Hungary, countries whose peoples have long resented—and occasionally resisted—incorporation into the Soviet empire.

In the event of war NATO should not permit Moscow to count upon their continued "loyalty." NATO should make it clear to Soviet leaders in advance that their forces in or passing through Eastern Europe will not enjoy a free ride— that they will be subjected to attacks ranging from deep aerial strikes to commando and partisan raids. To be more specific, NATO should develop the requisite special operations forces for the promotion and encouragement, *in the event of war*, of indigenous revolutionary violence against Soviet forces in the region. In the 1950s the United States trained and fielded special stay-behind forces dedicated to disrupting Soviet military activity in occupied territory and to promoting local popular resistance. Such forces should be revived; their very recreation would strengthen deterrence.

Many will argue that a declaratory policy of promoting revolution in Eastern Europe in wartime would be unsettling to a Soviet leadership already edgy about its future grip on Eastern Europe. The declared intention of such a policy, however, would not be to "roll back Communism" in Eastern Europe in peacetime, but rather to raise the risks and uncertainties confronting the Soviet military in wartime. Does anyone doubt that the Soviets under such circumstances would refrain from attempts to orchestrate "fifth column" activities in Western Europe?

A RIGID, CENTRALIZED COMMAND SYSTEM

A second Soviet military weakness lies in the incompatibility of its professed operational doctrine and its system of command authority. Whether on land, in the air, or at sea, rapid, opportunistic offensive operations designed to keep a defender always off balance by continually confronting him with a series of unexpected actions and appearances require a pervasive decentralization of command authority. Local commanders on the spot, governed only by broad, mission-type orders (which in essence tell a subordinate what to do but not how to do it), must be permitted the latitude of making critical decisions on their own since they are best able to assess the dangers, risks, and opportunities afforded by their immediate combat environment and can translate their judgment into action faster than commanders compelled to receive permission from higher authority.

Reliance on mission-type orders and decentralized command authority was the bedrock of the German Army's spectacular operational successes in World War II and has characterized Israeli military operations for over three decades. The exceptional speed and violence of modern warfare—the awesome rapidity with which expectations and even the best-laid plans can be overtaken by events— place a premium on exceptional flexibility at the tactical and operational levels of combat, a flexibility that can be had only through endowing subordinate commanders with exceptional authority. It goes without saying that decentralized command requires subordinate officers of high quality who are encouraged and willing to take the initiative.

The Soviet military professes an operational doctrine calling for rapid, unstinting (24-hour-a-day) offensive operations aimed at depriving an enemy of the initiative throughout the conflict.[2] Yet it is a military still governed by a comparatively rigid and centralized system of command authority, a system stemming from and constantly reinforced by an authoritarian political and ideological culture. Subordinate initiative not in conformity with the invariably detailed prescriptions of higher authority is not just discouraged, it is regarded as a challenge to the legitimacy of higher authority itself.

This internal contradiction between the decentralization of command authority required by the objective character of modern warfare and the centralization of command authority required by the subjective necessity to preserve the legitimacy of higher authority has served to reinforce allegiance to Russia's historic style of warfare: a heavy reliance on numbers as compensation for a persistent inability to adapt rapidly and effectively to unexpected events on the battlefield. Indeed, with some notable exceptions, operational rigidity has been the hallmark of the Soviet military performance in combat since the invasion of Finland in 1940. A ponderous methodicalness has been no less characteristic of the performance of most Third World militaries that are supplied, trained, and advised by the Soviet Union.

This is not to argue that debilitating inflexibility would inevitably characterize Soviet command and control in a future conflict. The Soviet military has not been called upon to wage a major conventional war since 1945 and has virtually no experience at all in combat on or under the high seas, thus denying U.S. and allied force planners any determinative referent experience. The present conflict in Afghanistan, in which Soviet military modernity is being pitted against an elusive, primitive foe under highly unfavorable local political conditions is of dubious instructiveness, although available information does suggest pervasive "micromanagement" of Soviet tactical operations from above and slow adaptation to the peculiar natural and operational conditions facing Soviet ground forces in that remote country.

To put it another way, there is no evidence that the Soviet military has resolved the contradiction between its traditional structure of command authority and the demands of its professed operational doctrine. If this is in fact the case, if the Soviet military, by virtue of its own traditional style of warfare and the singular political and ideological culture from which it is drawn, remains governed by a rigid and excessively centralized system of command authority, then the early disruption of that system in the event of war offers an indirect and potentially decisive means of dislocating Soviet operational plans and cohesion from the outset of hostilities. Indeed, the exceptional redundancy of, and protection afforded to, Soviet command, control, and communications could well be testimony to an overly centralized command system recognized by the Soviets themselves as a potential Achilles heel. The significance accorded by the Soviets to survivable command and control is no less evident in the heavy emphasis Soviet doctrine places on the early destruction of NATO's command and control.

To the extent that Soviet operational cohesion is unusually dependent upon an uninterrupted flow of orders and instructions from an unusually centralized chain of command authority, that chain should be a prime target of U.S. and allied force planning, even at the expense of resources currently dedicated to the destruction of Soviet combat forces. Paralyzing Soviet operations by going for the Soviet military's brain and central nervous system may be less costly than hacking away at its muscles, although it is not likely to be easier, given the redundancy of Soviet command, control, and communications.

Yet the task is not insurmountable. Specialized light ground forces dedicated to surprise penetration of Soviet rear areas, and new technologies, including cruise missiles and terminally guided precision and area submunitions, offer the prospect of rapid destruction of fixed and even mobile Soviet C^3 centers. It goes without saying that the effective application of such forces and technologies requires major improvements in NATO's current battlefield real-time intelligence-gathering and target-acquisition capabilities, together with improvements in the survivability of NATO's own C^3.

CONSTRAINED ACCESS TO THE SEA

A third Soviet military weakness deserving full exploitation by the West in the event of war is the Soviet Navy's difficult access to the open ocean. The very geography that works to the Soviet Union's advantage in a land war on the Eurasian landmass has conspired to place the Soviet Union at a distinct disadvantage in a naval war with the West. Indeed, the transformation of the Soviet Navy under Admiral Sergei Gorshkov from a coastal appendage of the land battle into a powerful "blue water" force may be regarded as an inherently unnatural development, as was Tirpitz's creation of a German High Seas Fleet in the decades before World War I. Like Wilhelmenian Germany, the Soviet Union is a continental power with continental military experiences and traditions. It possesses none of the basic elements of sea power, which Alfred Thayer Mahan defined as (1) "Geographical Position" (". . . if a nation be so situated that it is neither forced to defend itself by land nor induced to seek extension of its territory by way of the land, it has, by the very unity of its aim directed upon the sea, an advantage as compared with a people one of whose boundaries is continental"); (2) "Physical Conformation" (easy access to the sea); (3) "Extent of territory" (". . . not the total number of square miles which a country contains, but the length of its coastline and the character of its harbors . . ."); (4) "Number of Population" (". . . not only the grand total, but the number following the sea, or at least readily available for employment on shipboard . . ."); (5) "National Character" (". . . aptitude for commercial pursuits . . ."); and (6) "Character of the Government" (". . . in the matter of sea power, the most brilliant successes have followed where there has been intelligent direction by a government fully imbued with the spirit of the people and conscious of its true general bent. Such a Government is most certainly secured when the will of the people, or of their best natural exponents, have some large share in making it").[3]

To be sure, the Soviet Navy today, especially its large force of modern attack submarines, poses a major challenge to NATO's ability to maintain control of the sea in the event of war. Yet Western naval power, in terms of numbers of vessels, aggregate tonnage, and quality of individual ship design, continues to exceed that of the Soviet Union and its Warsaw Pact allies (the disparity in tonnage is attributable largely to America's 13 big-deck aircraft carriers, whose removal from the equation would substantially alter the balance). And although the wartime mission of the Soviet Navy (denial of sea control) is innately easier than NATO's (maintaining sea control), the former's lack of experience and geographical disadvantages are likely to prove telling in the event of war. The Russian Navy's last major combat experience was in the Russo-Japanese War of 1904–1905, which ended with Admiral Togo's destruction of virtually the entire Russian Baltic Fleet in the Battle of the Tsushima Strait. In World War I the Russian Fleet remained in port, serving as floating artillery batteries for adjacent land operations; in World War II the fleet again remained in home waters, providing fire support for ground operations and (in the case of the Black Sea Fleet) amphibious assault operations.

A major obstacle to Russian naval effectiveness then and now has been the lack of easy access to the high seas, which accounts in large measure for Moscow's centuries-old search for a warm-water port in unconfined waters. Like the German High Seas Fleet of 1914, whose access to the open ocean beyond the North Sea was severely limited by Great Britain's position astride the Channel and the North Sea narrows, the Soviet Navy's four separate fleets are separated from the high seas by a plethora of blockadable choke points. To reach the open ocean the Leningrad-based Baltic Fleet must pass through the narrow Danish Straits; the Sevastopol-based Black Sea Fleet must transit the even narrower Dardanelles (where it would still find itself in the Mediterranean—another sealable body of water); and the Vladivostok-based Pacific Fleet must break out of the confined waters of the Sea of Japan. Even the Murmansk-based Northern Fleet, which has relatively unconstrained access to the open ocean, must transit NATO's defensive barrier known as the Greenland-Iceland-United Kingdom (GIUK) gap. Only Soviet fleet units operating out of Petropavlovsk, on the Kamchatka Peninsula, have unimpeded access to the open ocean, although Petropavlovsk is a remote base that does not enjoy good land lines of communication with the Soviet interior.

The confined waters from which the Soviet Navy is compelled to operate afford NATO the opportunity to neutralize much of the striking power of the Soviet Navy without necessarily having to destroy that navy outright. Much would depend, of course, on the number of Russian vessels still in port when hostilities commenced; yet a blockade that effectively froze traffic to and from Soviet naval bases also would have obvious effects on the ability of Soviet warships already at sea to sustain combat. By locking the Soviet Navy up in— or out of—the Sea of Japan and in the Baltic, Black, and Norwegian Seas at the outset of hostilities, NATO could markedly reduce Moscow's potential challenge to vital Western maritime lines of communication in the Atlantic, Indian, and Pacific Oceans.

Admittedly implicit in such a strategy of "distant" blockade, similar to that pursued by the British Grand Fleet against the Imperial High Seas Fleet in World War I, would be the survival of much of the Soviet Navy and Soviet domination of the littorals of the Norwegian, Black, and Baltic Seas and the Sea of Japan. Yet, as British naval strategy demonstrated in World War I, gaining and maintaining command of the sea is not necessarily synonymous with the destruction of the challenger's navy. Moreover, given the Soviet submarine menace and the potency and reach of modern Soviet land-based air power dedicated to antinaval missions, a strategy aimed at crippling the Soviet Navy directly through carrier air strikes against its home bases could entail unacceptable U.S. and allied losses.

It also is to be recognized that even an early NATO victory at sea probably would not determine the outcome of the land battle in Europe. Although for NATO victory at sea is an indispensable condition for the successful prosecution of hostilities ashore in Europe, it is no guarantee of victory ashore.

Even if all Soviet ships were swept from the high seas and all Soviet home and overseas naval bases put out of action, could this prevent the U.S.S.R. from . . . overrunning Europe and the Middle East oil fields, emasculating or cowing China, or mounting a land-based missile and air threat to nearby Japan which would dwarf Hitler's 1944 V-1 and V-2 threat to wartime England? Sweeping up the Soviet navy, nibbling at the U.S.S.R.'s maritime flanks, even dealing with Soviet surrogates like

Cuba, South Yemen, Ethiopia and Vietnam would hardly suffice to prevent a great Eurasian heartland power like the U.S.S.R. from dominating our chief allies. . . .[4]

The issue, in sum, is neither the criticality of sea control to the West nor the imperative of exploiting the disadvantages imposed on Soviet naval operations by geography, both of which have long been recognized by U.S. naval force planners and strategists, but rather the best means of gaining and keeping control of the sea. A strategy aimed at destroying the Soviet Navy in its own waters risks losses far outweighing potential gains. The alternative is a strategy aimed at confining the Soviet naval vessels to their own waters and starving the rest on the high seas. As the astute naval writer Herbert Rosinski observed in 1939, blockade is

> . . . a *form* of command [of the sea], because—although with many imperfections— it fulfills its function of excluding our opponent from the use of the sea. Thus it is blockade which really constitutes the corner-stone of naval warfare, while the fuller measure of command achieved by the complete destruction of the enemy's main forces forms merely its superstructure.[5]

FRAGILE EAST–WEST LINES OF COMMUNICATION

A fourth Soviet weakness is the comparatively fragile land lines of communication between European Russia and the Soviet Far East. Roughly one-third of the Soviet Union's ground and tactical air forces are deployed in the Far East. Their transfer to Europe in the event of a NATO–Warsaw Pact conflict on the Continent would provide the Pact an overwhelming preponderance of force against which even the strongest NATO defenses could not possibly hold. On the other hand, given the size of Soviet ground and tactical air forces deployed west of the Urals, it is not certain that Moscow would need to transfer substantial forces from the Far East to Europe to ensure victory in Europe. Certainly the key to Soviet success in a major conflict confined to the Far East would be the timely transfer of forces now deployed in European Russia.

It is worth recalling that failure to complete the trans-Siberian railroad until after the outbreak of the Russo-Japanese War in 1904 accounted in no small measure for Russia's defeat in that conflict by making it impossible to transfer her vastly larger forces to the arena of combat. It is also worth remembering that completion of that railroad and its subsequent expansion into a double-track line permitted Stalin in 1941 to move no fewer than 18 crack Siberian divisions to the West, thereby ensuring a successful defense of Moscow against the German onslaught.

The trans-Siberian railroad nevertheless remains the only land link between European Russia and the Far East; there are no roads connecting eastern and western Russia, and the arctic maritime route is passable for only about 160 days a year. Moreover, from Lake Baykal to Vladivostok much of the trans-Siberian lies uncomfortably close to China (at several points the line runs within 50 kilometers of the border). It is in part for this reason that the Soviets have undertaken construction of a second rail line running north of Lake Baykal to Amur, although the Baykal-Amur (BAM) line will not fully resolve the potential threat of interdiction posed by China.

Exploitation of the Soviet Union's comparatively fragile east-west land lines of communication would not be easy in the event of war, although the pay-off for success could be decisive. The history of modern warfare has shown that, even under the most intense aerial bombardment, rail networks are difficult to shut down for more than a few days; destroyed tracks and road beds are easily repaired; blasted railroad bridges can often be replaced by specially configured pontoon spans; and tunnels deep underground are virtually impossible to collapse from above with standard conventional munitions. The Soviet Army, moreover, maintains over 100,000 specialized railroad troops dedicated to the construction of railroads in peacetime and their repair and maintenance in wartime.

On the other hand, such new technologies as improved conventional munitions and long-range sea-launched cruise missiles offer the prospect of substantially disrupting rail traffic by destroying selected critical bridges (those traversing gorges, for example), tunnels, and other comparatively difficult-to-replace components of the rail system. Nor should the potential of properly conceived special operations against the trans-Siberian be discounted.

The Soviet Union does not enjoy the advantages of interior lines of communication with respect to the Far Eastern "front." On the contrary, the United States can move, from its western coast via the Pacific, more military power, and move it faster, to the Far East than can the Soviet Union. For this reason, the region should be—and increasingly is—regarded as one of great potential operational opportunity in the event of a worldwide war with the Soviet Union. The trans-Siberian should be viewed as an internal choke point whose "blockade" could affect the outcome of the land war as much as a blockade of the Danish Straits, Dardanelles, GIUK gap, and Sea of Japan could affect the outcome of the war at sea.

TECHNOLOGICAL INFERIORITY

Much has been made in recent years of the success the Soviet Union has enjoyed in eliminating, and in some cases surpassing, longstanding Western qualitative advantages in conventional weaponry, especially in those technologies associated with the land battle—armored fighting vehicles, antitank weapons, artillery, armed helicopters, and battlefield air defenses. There is no doubt that the once-marked margin of technological superiority upon which the West for so long relied as a means of partially offsetting the Soviet Union's advantage in numbers has been significantly narrowed during the past decade and a half.

On balance, however, the Warsaw Pact remains technologically inferior to NATO, despite a rather casual and often inadvertent transfer to the Soviet Union of Western technologies suitable for military application. This inferiority is particularly notable in technologies associated with warfare at sea and in the air, and with advanced conventional munitions and their delivery. To be sure, the Soviet Navy is no longer a coastal defense force, and today reflects major and impressive technological advances. Yet, ship for ship, U.S. vessels still possess more fighting power and endurance than their Soviet counterparts, and when respective allied navies are factored into the naval balance, NATO continues to enjoy a numerical advantage over the Warsaw Pact, an advantage that is immeasurably heightened by NATO's comparatively easy access to the high seas.

And, to be sure, Soviet frontal aviation has been transformed from a short-range, low-payload, interceptor force dedicated to the defense of Warsaw Pact air space into a long-range, large-payload, offensive force capable of carrying the air war deep into NATO territory. Yet, if the 1982 Syrian-Israeli air war over Lebanon is any measure, modern Soviet tactical aircraft remain decidedly inferior to the best U.S. planes. No doubt it was the combination of better aircraft, tactical and operational ingenuity, and the vastly superior quality of Israeli pilots (whose combat experience and level of training are probably unmatched anywhere in the world) that underlay one of the most lopsided air battles in history.

Here, too, however, the conflict in Lebanon was perhaps more instructive than apparent at first glance. Air-to-air combat places a heavy premium upon individual initiative, decentralized command and control at the tactical level, and upon flexibility and opportunism in the application of violence—virtues that are not effectively promoted within the Soviet military, and that certainly have not been evident in the performance of most Soviet-model client armies. The abysmal performance of the Syrian air forces in 1982 was in large measure attributable to a rigid, centralized control of air operations from the ground and an excessive reliance on preconceived plans and tactics unable to keep pace with rapidly altering reality.

No less significant is that, unlike the Syrian Air Force, the Soviet Air Force has comparatively little combat experience (only a tiny fraction of Soviet frontal aviation is being employed in Afghanistan); but that, like Syrian pilots, Soviet pilots on balance receive substantially less training (certainly in terms of flying hours) than do their counterparts in the West. Additionally, the Soviet military is plagued by serious racial, ethnic, and religious divisions within the enlisted ranks and between the largely Slavic officer corps and an increasingly non-Slavic rank-and-file. These divisions, which are likely to widen as the Slavic portion of the Soviet Union's population continues its relative decline, raise

> . . . important questions about the reliability of the army under certain conditions,
> such as possible combat operations against neighboring Moslem and Asian countries,
> on the use of military force to suppress ethnic-based domestic unrest.[6]

In short, NATO retains over the Warsaw Pact a significant qualitative superiority in most naval and aerial conventional weaponry, a superiority that is enhanced by greater combat experience and social cohesion, and by a generally higher investment in the training of personnel operating that weaponry.

This is not to suggest that the Warsaw Pact's technological inferiority at sea and in the air would be decisive in a future conflict in Europe, although it could well be in the Pacific and even Persian Gulf theaters of operations. The Alliance's margin of qualitative superiority in both men and weapons has never been sufficient, alone, to offset the Pact's numerical, operational, and geographic advantages with respect to a war in Europe and in other areas on the Eurasian landmass adjacent to the Soviet empire. Technology is, in any event, but one of a multitude of influences at work on the battlefield, and rarely the decisive one. The history of warfare even in this century shows that wars are still decided primarily by numbers and by such intangible factors as leadership, strategy, tactics, morale, unit cohesion, and just plain luck. (Would the ultimate outcome of the Israeli-Syrian conflict of 1982 have been any different had both countries exchanged their respective inventories of weapons before the outbreak of hostilities?)

Yet to argue that NATO's technological superiority in the air and at sea is not likely to be decisive is not to argue that it is insignificant or expendable. On the contrary, while technological superiority alone is no recipe for victory, failure to maintain, and if possible to increase, that superiority would make defeat highly probable. As a coalition of democratic societies politically sensitive to heavy casualties on the battlefield (a sensitivity that markedly influenced Britain's operational planning pursuant to its reconquest of the Falklands in 1982), NATO has long emphasized the substitution of firepower for manpower, machines for men. Moreover, there can be no question that technological advantage does in some measure offset the Warsaw Pact's advantage in numbers; certainly a combination of technological and numerical inferiority would doom NATO to almost certain defeat in the event of war.

It is, therefore, imperative that the West retain the qualitative advantages it still enjoys at sea and in the air, and that it strive, where possible, to increase those advantages and create new ones. This is especially true with respect to naval and tactical air power. Outnumbered and outgunned U.S. and allied ground forces cannot hope to prevail in the absence of air superiority at least over the battle area, and without controlling the seas behind them; and the inherent flexibility and mobility of naval and tactical air power make them essential ingredients to successful intervention in such logistically remote areas as Southwest Asia.

It should go without saying that attempts to preserve remaining technological advantages over the Warsaw Pact are ill-served by the continuing leakage of militarily applicable Western technology to the Warsaw Pact. To be sure, almost every advanced technology lends itself to some form of military application; even U.S. grain sales to the Soviet Union, by in effect subsidizing the weakest sector of the Soviet economy, permit internal reallocations of resources into Moscow's military machine. On the other hand, some technologies are distinctly more applicable than others, and commercial profits are not always synonymous with the national security interest. The machinery for tighter regulation of technology transfer to the Warsaw Pact already exists in the form of the Coordinating Committee, which was created in the early 1950s; what is needed is greater political resolve to make it work.

NOTES

1. Jones, "What's Wrong with Our Defense Establishment," pp. 70–71.
2. For a comprehensive expatiation of extant Soviet military doctrine and thought, see the continuing series of works, "Soviet Military Thought," in particular A. A. Sidorenko, *The Offensive (A Soviet View)* (1970); V. Ye Savkin, *The Basic Principles of Operational Art and Tactics* (1972); and N. A. Lomov, *Scientific-Technical Progress and the Revolution in Military Affairs* (1973), all translated and published under the auspices of the U.S. Air Force (Washington, D.C.: U.S. Government Printing Office, 1973, 1974, and 1974, respectively). See also Joseph D. Douglass, Jr., *Soviet Military Strategy in Europe* (New York: Pergamon Press, 1980); and Christopher N. Donnelly, "Soviet Operational Concepts in the 1980s," in *Strengthening Conventional Defense, Proposals for the 1980s*, Report of the European Security Study (New York: St. Martins Press, 1983), pp. 105–136.
3. Alfred Thayer Mahan, *The Influence of Sea Power upon History, 1660–1783* (Boston: Little, Brown and Company, 1890), pp. 29–89.
4. Robert W. Komer, "Maritime Strategy vs. Coalition Defense," *Foreign Affairs* (Summer, 1982), pp. 1133–1134.
5. B. Mitchell Simpson III, *The Development of Naval Thought, Essays by Herbert Rosinski* (Newport: Naval War College Press, 1977), p. 6.
6. Coit D. Blacker, "Military Forces," in Robert F. Byrnes, ed., *After Brezhnev, Sources of Soviet Conduct in the 1980s* (Bloomington: Indiana University Press, 1983), p. 50.

CHAPTER 9.
GREATER RELIANCE ON RESERVE FORCES

Another means of bringing U.S. military capabilities and obligations into closer alignment is greater reliance on reserve forces. Reserve forces, if properly trained, equipped, supported, and integrated with active forces, are perhaps the best defense bargain available, and could even permit a modest reduction in far more expensive active-duty forces.

For the United States, greater reliance on reserve forces is likely to be unavoidable. The American male population of military age, both in absolute number and as a percentage of the population as a whole, is declining and will continue to decline well into the 1990s; by 1993, the number of 19-year-old American males will drop from the present 2,086,000 to 1,622,000. This trend will make it increasingly difficult for the All-Volunteer Force to recruit and retain manpower sufficient to meet even current authorized service end-strengths without a significant reduction in quality, or major increases in pay, benefits, and other personnel costs, which already consume over one-half of the defense budget. The current boom in recruiting is likely to be short-lived, since it is fueled primarily by high unemployment in the civilian sector. Indeed, the combination of adverse demographic trends and economic recovery could dictate a return to conscription by the end of the decade, smaller standing forces, or even both. Conscription, in addition to solving the problem of active-duty force recruitment, also has proven the most effective promoter of reserve recruitment.

It should be noted in passing that militarily adverse demographic trends confront U.S. NATO allies as well, especially the Federal Republic of Germany. The government of Helmut Kohl is weighing a number of options designed to maintain the *Bundeswehr*'s current end-strength (approximately 495,000) through the early 1990s. Even if adopted, however, those options, which include lengthening the initial term of military obligation for recruits, tightening requirements for conscientious objection, and greater reliance on women in noncombat military occupational specialties, are likely to be inadequate. Reductions on the order of 30,000 to 50,000 personnel appear unavoidable by the latter 1980s.

Countries as disparate as Israel, Sweden, the Netherlands, and Yugoslavia, all of whom rely on conscription, have shown what can be done with properly trained, equipped, and integrated reserve forces; and it is significant that the Soviets themselves have staggered the readiness of their conscripted ground forces according to anticipated wartime need while at the same time achieving a high level of coordination between their fully active and cadred units. It is equally significant that the United States continues to maintain at home a level of active-duty forces, especially ground forces, that far exceeds existing capacity to deploy them overseas in a timely fashion. Moreover, the Air National Guard and some Army National Guard units have repeatedly demonstrated that it is possible to maintain a degree of readiness and performance equivalent to that of their active-duty counterparts.

All of this suggests that intelligently staggered and integrated active and reserve forces could yield the United States a less costly yet more combat-effective force structure characterized by smaller standing forces but larger, readier reserve components. The time has come to stop parroting the virtues of the Total Force concept and make it a reality. The real price of continuing to starve reserve forces in order to feed the active forces is a sharply segregated and disjointed force structure, whose aggregate effectiveness is less than that of the sum of its parts.

It is also to be noted that NATO Europe possesses an enormous pool of trained reservists, only a tiny fraction of which have been organized into combat units. Belgium, France, the Netherlands, and Germany alone have a total of over 1.1 million army reservists, and each year release about 500,000 conscripts after 8 to 17 months of active duty.[1] Most, however, are assigned to individual replacement pools rather than to organized units, thereby diluting substantially their mobilizable combat potential. At least one analyst has concluded that "Western Europe has the wherewithal to create the forces necessary for its own defense,"[2] if only it would take proper advantage of its trained reservists. Another has charged that the "retention of American active forces in [the United States] primarily to reinforce NATO, instead of equipping existing European reserve forces to accomplish the same mission, must be the most flagrant instance of waste, fraud, and free-loading in alliance security efforts."[3] There can be no doubt that the combat potential of European reservists far exceeds that of the three U.S. divisions to be withdrawn from Europe as part of the new transatlantic division of military labor proposed in this study.

NOTES

1. William P. Mako, *U.S. Ground Forces and the Defense of Central Europe* (Washington, D.C.: The Brookings Institution, 1983), p. 89.
2. Steven I. Canby, *Short (And Long) War Responses: Restructuring, Border Defense, and Reserve Mobilization for Armored Warfare*, prepared for the U.S. Department of Defense, Director of Special Studies (Santa Monica, Calif.: Technology Service Corp., 1978), p. 88. See also Kenneth Hunt, *The Alliance and Europe, pt. 2: Defense with Fewer Men*, Adelphi Paper 98 (London: International Institute for Strategic Studies, 1973).
3. Sullivan, "The Real Long-Range Defense Dilemma: Burden Sharing," p. 90.

CHAPTER 10.
ENHANCED STRATEGIC MOBILITY

As noted in Part I, nowhere is the gap between U.S. military power and obligations wider than in the area of strategic mobility. Strategic mobility is vital to the military effectiveness of the United States, which is separated from its primary defense commitments by thousands of miles of water. Forces in the United States that cannot be moved overseas when and where they are needed are forces whose potential contribution to the outcome of combat is severely degraded.

Since the 1950s, however, the United States has never maintained air- and sealift capabilities sufficient to meet NATO-related deployment requirements, despite increasing reliance on the prepositioning of division sets of equipment ashore in Europe. The recent commitment of U.S. military power to the defense of more distant Southwest Asia, where the option of prepositioning ashore is denied, has served only to inflate substantially what was already a significant shortfall between forces slated for movement and means of moving them.

This chronic shortfall, which in actuality eliminates from the East-West conventional military balance those forces stationed in the United States but not deployable in a timely fashion, is attributable to several factors. Strategic mobility, and especially airlift, is very expensive; the program unit cost (in fiscal 1983 dollars) of each of the 50 new C-5B air transports the Reagan Administration intends to procure amounts to $115.9 million; and that of the 60–72 KC-10 tanker/cargo aircraft, $55.6 million. Military shipping, ranging from amphibious vessels to fast-deployment logistics ships to maritime prepositioning ships, also is expensive.

A second reason is that strategic lift has always been a stepchild in the Pentagon. None of the armed services likes to spend precious procurement dollars on items designed primarily to help other services accomplish their missions; most Air Force senior officers would much rather spend money on warplanes than on transport aircraft, although airlift is essential to the early projection of U.S. ground forces *and* tactical airpower overseas (indeed, the U.S. Air Force has first claim on Military Airlift Command assets in a deployment crisis); likewise, the Navy traditionally has resisted all but minimal investment in amphibious shipping, which is vital to the prosecution of the Marine Corps' principal mission. It is no coincidence that the Army and the Marine Corps, the two services most dependent upon strategic lift, are the two services most supportive of life enhancement programs. Seemingly forgotten by both the Air Force and the Navy is the Anglo-American experience of World War II, in which the timing and character of combined operations in both Europe and the Pacific were adversely constrained by chronic shortages in shipping (especially amphibious shipping) and tactical airlift, shortages attributable in no small measure to the procurement parochialism of both services.

A third factor is strategic mobility's association, in the minds of many in the Congress and much of the American public, with undesirable military intervention in distant Third World areas where the United States is perceived to enjoy no vital interests. Some believe that the best way to avoid another Vietnam is simply to deny the Pentagon the tools of intervention in such areas; a strategically immobile Rapid Deployment Force may be a contradiction in terms, but it would undeniably warm the hearts of those persuaded either that Southwest Asia is but another Vietnam writ large, or that the Pentagon is infested by warmongers constantly chaffing at the bit for opportunities to practice their trade.

To be sure, strategic mobility enhancement programs now under way[1] will substantially reduce the gap between lift requirements and capabilities. Yet, given the continuing fragility of strategic lift's military constituency and mounting political pressures of a deficit-shocked Congress on "marginal" Pentagon procurement programs, there is no assurance that any or all of these programs will be adequately funded to completion in the latter 1980s. Moreover, even were they fully funded the United States would still suffer a significant shortfall in the strategic lift necessary to conduct simultaneous deployments to Europe and the Persian Gulf, to say nothing of meeting the lift requirements of the Reagan Administration's "worldwide war" strategy. The shortfall would be especially evident in airlift: The Joint Chiefs of Staff have stated that although completion of current airlift programs would increase current lift capacity from 30 million-ton-miles (MTM) per day to 46 MTM per day by 1989, there would still be a shortfall against *minimum* requirements of some 20 MTM, or 30 percent.[2]

Additional strategic lift, over and above that to be provided by current programs, is clearly needed if the United States is to be able to meet its expanded overseas military commitments. Indeed, a strong case can be made for enhancing strategic mobility even at the expense of forces slated for movement. A U.S.-based rapidly deployable and combat effective Army or Marine Corps division is worth more than two strategically immobile ones, and, if the price of additional strategic lift is a reduction elsewhere in the force structure, the price should be paid.

Like current lift programs, new lift initiatives will have to grapple with the question of how best to allocate mobility dollars on the margin between sealift and airlift. There can be no question that flying military forces and materiel from one place to another is vastly more expensive than moving them by water or land, or having them already prepositioned in areas of potential crisis. Surface transportation is cheaper and can move infinitely larger forces. The value of airlift derives from situations in which one or more of the following circumstances apply: (1) surface transportation is unavailable, inadequate, or denied (e.g.,

Soviet closure of surface access to Berlin in 1948–1949); (2) delivery must be accomplished quickly, at a speed exceeding that of surface transportation (e.g., Israel's immediate need for antitank missiles and other "smart" munitions in the October War of 1973); and (3) prepositioning of necessary forces and materiel ahead of time in areas of anticipated need is impossible or undesirable (e.g., Southwest Asia today). Airlift is, of course, also essential to the insertion of combat forces by parachute or air-landing operations.

The value of robust airlift capabilities is obvious with respect to potential contingencies in Southwest Asia, where the United States does not enjoy politically secure military access ashore, and where events justifying the invocation of American military power are likely to occur with a degree of warning insufficient to guarantee the timely arrival of initial U.S. forces by sea. This is not to belittle the deterrent or war-fighting value of on-station sea power, maritime prepositioning, or sealift: As argued earlier, all are essential to any credible Rapid Deployment Force and certainly to a sea-based RDF of the kind proposed in this study, and would be vital in sustaining any conflict that lasted more than two or three weeks. Airlift, however, can do things that sealift cannot, and the peculiar political and operational environments confronting the United States in Southwest Asia place a premium on airlift's inherent virtues of speed, flexibility, and ability to deliver forces directly to places deep inland.

What is needed is an across-the-board expansion in U.S. airlift, fast sealift, and amphibious shipping capacity beyond that now contemplated. Sustaining such an expansion will require greater public and congressional appreciation of the fact that America's comparative geographic isolation from most potential military threats facing the Western World dictates an unparalleled investment in strategic mobility if the United States is to play the leading role in countering those threats. Also required will be the elimination of strategic lift's stepchild status within the Pentagon. It has been suggested that the only sure way of providing strategic lift the military constituency it deserves would be to disband the present service-controlled lift commands and to establish a fifth armed service, on an equal footing with the Army, Navy, Air Force, and Marine Corps, dedicated exclusively to the provision of strategic mobility. This suggestion should be thoroughly explored by a blue ribbon commission free of domination by parochial service interests.

It ought to go without saying that effective lift expansion would be facilitated by coordination between the Army and Air Force with respect to ensuring compatibility between lift aircraft and the principal items of hardware slated for movement. Unfortunately, the design of much of the Army's past and present equipment, and especially tanks and armored fighting vehicles such as the current M-1 Abrams main battle tank and Bradley Fighting Vehicle, reflects a gross insensitivity to the weight and space limitations of both the C-141 and C-5A/B strategic air transports. Given the vastly greater unit cost of strategic airlift (the cost of a C-5B is 25 times that of the Abrams tank), it is far more cost-effective to design tanks and fighting vehicles to accommodate lift aircraft than vice versa. The Army is, encouragingly, becoming increasingly aware of this problem and is exploring new lightweight armored vehicle designs suitable for rapid deployment by air.

NOTES

1. Sealift programs include: (1) increasing the Ready Reserve Fleet from 29 to 77 ships, including 61 dry-cargo ships and 16 tankers; (2) conversion of 8 fast SL-7 roll-on/roll-off vessels to deploy Army combat and support forces; and (3) procurement of 13 specially designed Maritime Prepositioning Ships to preposition equipment afloat in the Indian Ocean for three Marine Amphibious Brigades. Airlift programs include procurement of (1) 50 additional C-5B aircraft; and (2) 60–72 KC-10 tanker/cargo aircraft.
2. *United States Military Posture, FY 1984*, prepared by the Organization of the Joint Chiefs of Staff (Washington, D.C.: U.S. Government Printing Office, 1983), p. 50.

CHAPTER 11.
LOOKING FORWARD

Bringing U.S. conventional military aspirations and resources into reasonable harmony is no mean task. But it is a task that must be pursued with utmost vigor in an era of international nuclear stalemate, expanding Soviet military power, and increasing U.S. dependence on vital energy and mineral deposits in logistically remote and politically unstable areas of the world. To its credit, the Reagan Administration has recognized the dangers inherent in the strategy/force mismatch it inherited, and has sought to narrow the gap between U.S. commitments and capabilities by expanding the latter. More, much more, however, needs to be done.

The relative economic and military weight of the United States in the world at large has steadily declined in the postwar era, and its subsequent loss of decisive nuclear superiority over the Soviet Union—a superiority not likely to be reestablished in our lifetime (if ever)—has vastly inflated the political and military significance of longstanding Western deficiencies in conventional military power, in which the Soviet Union has enjoyed a preponderance on the Eurasian landmass since 1945. Actual or threatened U.S. nuclear responses to non-nuclear aggression are no longer credible, making robust and comparatively expensive conventional defenses the imperative centerpiece of future attempts to contain Soviet and Soviet-sponsored military expansion.

Western recognition of these harsh realities has been slow and uneven. In Europe, which remains the principal and single most critical arena of East–West military competition and confrontation despite the proliferation of Soviet threats outside the North Atlantic area, key allies continue to exhibit a nostalgic and unwarranted confidence in the U.S. nuclear deterrent as a means both of preventing war and of excusing all but token efforts on their part to remedy NATO's conventional force weaknesses. This confidence has been attended in many quarters by a determination to believe that the Soviet Union has become a benign state, wracked by internal economic, social, and political problems precluding malignant international behavior in the future.

Despite its larger population base and greater aggregate economic power, NATO Europe still devotes relatively far less of its resources to the common defense than does the United States, which continues to bear the primary burden of defending Western interests both in Europe and outside the NATO Treaty area. No less disturbing is the failure of many European decision-makers to appreciate the connection between a continuation of inequitable burden-sharing and a potentially resurgent and triumphant neoisolationism in the United States, signs of which are already evident in the Congress.

All of this is, to be sure, unfortunate, because the central foundation of any attempt to harmonize U.S. (and for that matter, Western) military aspirations and resources lies in a level of allied investment more commensurate with allied economic power and a new division of military labor within the West along functional and geographic lines. In the absence of greater allied defense investment and a new division of military labor, even full realization of all of the other measures proposed in this study would leave the United States still facing a profound gap between its military commitments and capabilities.

The real question is what it has always been within the Atlantic Alliance: Can the Alliance muster the political will to do what is militarily necessary to ensure its survival?

APPENDIX A

U.S. Defense Budget Trends, Fiscal Years 1950–1988 (In billions of fiscal year 1983 dollars)

YEAR	BUDGET AUTHORITY		OUTLAYS	
	AMOUNT	% CHANGE	AMOUNT	% CHANGE
1950	79.4		69.1	
1951	224.5	+182.9	107.3	+55.3
1952	288.8	+28.6	193.9	+80.7
1953	235.0	−18.6	207.3	+6.9
1954	175.9	−25.1	194.9	−6.0
1955	149.5	−15.0	168.4	−13.6
1956	153.6	+2.7	162.5	−3.5
1957	163.2	+6.3	166.5	+2.5
1958	159.6	−2.2	162.7	−2.3
1959	170.9	+7.1	165.4	+1.7
1960	166.0	−2.8	164.3	−0.7
1961	165.5	−0.3	166.9	+1.6
1962	188.5	+13.9	179.6	+7.7
1963	191.8	+1.7	182.6	+1.6
1964	184.6	−3.7	181.6	−0.6
1965	177.7	−4.1	165.6	−8.8
1966	213.1	+20.4	183.2	+10.7
1967	232.3	+9.0	216.1	+18.0
1968	235.4	+1.3	236.0	+9.2
1969	226.5	−3.8	229.6	−2.7
1970	204.4	−9.7	211.6	−7.8
1971	183.8	−10.1	191.9	−9.3
1972	178.9	−2.7	179.4	−6.5
1973	170.8	−4.5	164.0	−8.6
1974	165.2	−3.3	160.5	−2.1
1975	161.5	−2.3	160.6	+0.1
1976	168.2	+4.2	155.1	−3.4
1977	177.2	+5.3	157.9	+1.8
1978	174.2	−1.7	158.7	+0.5
1979	174.4	+0.1	165.0	+3.9
1980	178.3	+2.3	170.0	+3.0
1981	200.3	+12.3	177.8	+4.6
1982	223.8	+11.7	191.1	+7.5
1983	239.4	+7.0	208.9	+9.3
1984*	263.6	+10.1	230.2	+10.2
1985*	292.6	+11.0	252.1	+9.5
1986*	308.4	+5.4	271.8	+7.8
1987*	320.7	+4.0	284.8	+4.8
1988*	333.5	+4.0	295.8	+3.9

Source: *Defense Spending and the Economy* (Washington, D.C.: Congressional Budget Office, 1983).

* Planned by the Reagan Administration.

APPENDIX B

U.S. Defense Outlays as a Percentage of Federal Spending and Gross
National Product, 1940–1982

FISCAL YEAR	% OF FEDERAL BUDGET	% OF GNP
1940	15.8	1.6
1941	44.3	5.5
1942	71.0	17.9
1943	83.6	37.1
1944	85.5	38.7
1945	88.3	37.3
1946	17.3	20.6
1947	33.6	5.2
1948	26.3	3.2
1949	30.3	4.5
1950	29.1	4.7
1951	48.0	7.0
1952	64.0	12.8
1953	65.6	13.8
1954	65.3	12.7
1955	58.1	10.5
1956	56.4	9.7
1957	55.3	9.8
1958	52.9	9.9
1959	49.9	9.7
1960	49.0	9.1
1961	47.7	9.2
1962	45.9	9.0
1963	45.0	8.7
1964	43.5	8.4
1965	40.1	7.2
1966	40.7	7.6
1967	43.1	8.8
1968	44.0	9.5
1969	43.0	8.8
1970	40.0	8.2
1971	35.9	7.4
1972	33.0	6.9
1973	30.2	6.0
1974	28.8	5.7
1975	26.2	5.0
1976	24.4	5.5
1977	24.2	5.3
1978	23.3	5.1
1979	23.8	5.1
1980	23.4	5.3
1981	24.7	5.7
1982	27.2	5.9

Source: Caspar W. Weinberger, *Annual Report to the Congress for Fiscal Year 1983* (Washington, D.C.: Department of Defense, 1982).

APPENDIX C

U.S. Army Active-Duty Personnel End-Strengths and Divisions, Fiscal Years
1945–1982

YEAR	PERSONNEL END STRENGTHS	NUMBER OF DIVISIONS
1945	8,266,373	89
1946	1,889,690	16
1947	989,664	12
1948	554,030	11
1949	660,473	10
1950	593,167	10
1951	1,531,596	18
1952	1,596,419	20
1953	1,533,815	20
1954	1,404,598	19
1955	1,109,296	20
1956	1,025,778	18
1957	997,994	18
1958	898,925	15
1959	861,964	15
1960	873,078	14
1961	858,622	14
1962	1,066,404	14
1963	975,916	16
1964	973,238	16
1965	969,066	16
1966	1,199,784	17
1967	1,442,498	17
1968	1,570,343	19
1969	1,512,169	18
1970	1,322,548	16
1971	1,123,810	13
1972	810,959	13
1973	801,015	13
1974	783,330	13
1975	784,333	14
1976	779,417	16
1977	782,246	16
1978	771,624	16
1979	758,852	16
1980	777,036	16
1981	781,419	16
1982	780,753	16

Source: Information provided to the author by the Department of the Army.

APPENDIX D

U.S. Navy Active-Duty Personnel End-Strengths, Combatant Ships, and Fleet Carriers in Commission, Fiscal Years 1945–1983

YEAR	PERSONNEL END STRENGTHS	COMBATANTS	FLEET CARRIERS
1945	3,380,817	4,503	98*
1946	983,398	780	26
1947	498,661	625	21
1948	419,162	641	21
1949	449,575	457	18
1950	381,538	447	15
1951	736,680	789	26
1952	824,265	831	29
1953	794,440	843	29
1954	725,720	824	26
1955	660,695	769	24
1956	669,925	737	24
1957	677,108	743	22
1958	641,005	677	24
1959	626,340	655	23
1960	617,984	615	23
1961	627,089	624	24
1962**	666,428	754**	26
1963	664,647	752	24
1964	667,596	751	24
1965	671,448	769	25
1966	745,205	794	23
1967	751,619	811	23
1968	765,457	811	23
1969	775,869	769	22
1970	692,660	650	19
1971	623,248	571	18
1972	588,043	556	17
1973	564,534	496	16
1974	545,903	440	14
1975	535,085	437	15
1976	527,781	421	13
1977	529,895	414	13
1978	530,253	417	13
1979	523,937	420	13
1980	527,352	422	13
1981	540,504	423	12
1982	553,196	439	13
1983		425	13

Source: Information provided to the author by the Department of the Navy.

* Includes carriers of all types.

** Figures for years after 1961 includes combatant ships in the reserve mobilization forces.

APPENDIX E

U.S. Air Force Active-Duty Personnel End-Strengths, Tactical Combat Wings, and Aircraft, Fiscal Years 1947–1982

YEAR	PERSONNEL END STRENGTHS	TACTICAL WINGS	AIRCRAFT
1947	305,827	24 Groups*	7,965
1948	387,730	25	4,425
1949	419,347	20	3,862
1950	411,277	20	4,198
1951	788,381	18	4,722
1952	982,361	15 Wings	4,993
1953	977,593	16	5,881
1954	947,918	21	6,984
1955	959,946	23	9,519
1956	909,958	28	8,036
1957	919,835	25	7,115
1958	871,156	24	6,054
1959	840,435	18	5,501
1960	814,752	18	4,787
1961	821,151	25	4,074
1962	884,111	22	3,921
1963	869,576	21	3,721
1964	856,890	22	3,808
1965	824,709	23	3,761
1966	887,441	25	3,600
1967	897,426	26	3,914
1968	904,759	28	4,169
1969	862,062	24	3,681
1970	791,078	78 Squadrons**	3,269
1971	755,107	71	2,877
1972	725,635	63	2,391
1973	690,999	74	2,408
1974	643,795	74	2,009
1975	612,551	70	1,984
1976	585,207	73	2,196
1977	570,479	76	2,311
1978	569,491	78	2,370
1979	559,220	79	2,308
1980	557,969	78	2,360
1981	570,302	78	2,442
1982	582,845	79	2,442

Source: Information provided to the author by the Department of the Air Force.

* Echelon most closely related to a wing. It was not until June, 1952, that the Air Force's strength was stated in terms of wings rather than groups.

** Beginning in 1970, combat units have been reported in terms of squadrons.

APPENDIX F

U.S. Military Personnel in the European Command (EU-
COM) Geographical Area, 1950–1982*

YEAR	NUMBER
1950	145,000
1951	346,000
1952	405,000
1953	427,000
1954	404,000
1955	405,000
1956	398,000
1957	393,000
1958	380,000
1959	380,000
1960	379,000
1961	417,000
1962	416,000
1963	380,000
1964	374,000
1965	363,000
1966	366,000
1967	337,000
1968	316,000
1969	300,000
1970	291,000
1971	303,000
1972	307,000
1973	300,000
1974	300,000
1975	303,000
1976	308,000
1977	318,000
1978	325,000
1979	330,000
1980	323,000
1981	329,000
1982	329,000

Source: Information provided by the Department of Defense to the United States Senate, reprinted in the
Congressional Record (Senate) (May 12, 1982), p. S4992.

* Includes Army, Air Force, Navy (ashore and afloat),
and Marine Corps (ashore and afloat). Includes small
numbers of U.S. military personnel in non-NATO countries in the EUCOM geographical area such as Spain,
Austria, Switzerland, and until 1982, Spain.

BIBLIOGRAPHY

Books

Betts, Richard K. *Surprise Attack, Lessons for Defense Planning*. Washington, D.C.: The Brookings Institution, 1982.

Blackett, P.M.S. *Studies of War, Nuclear and Conventional*. London: Oliver and Boyd, 1962.

Brown, Harold. *Thinking About National Security, Defense and Foreign Policy in a Dangerous World*. Boulder, Colo.: Westview Press, 1983.

Brzezinski, Zbigniew. *Power and Principle, Memoirs of the National Security Advisor 1977–1981*. New York: Farrar, Straus and Giroux, 1983.

Canby, Steven L. *Short (And Long) War Responses: Restructuring, Border Defense, and Reserve Mobilization for Armored Warfare*. Santa Monica: Technology Service Corporation, 1978.

Clausewitz, Karl von. *On War*. Edited and translated by Michael Howard and Peter Paret with Introductory Essays by Peter Paret, Michael Howard, and Bernard Brodie. Princeton: Princeton University Press, 1976.

Close, Robert. *Europe Without Defense? 48 Hours That Could Change the Face of the World*. New York: Pergamon Press, 1979.

Coffey, Kenneth J. *Strategic Implications of the All-Volunteer Force: The Conventional Defense of Europe*. Chapel Hill: University of North Carolina Press, 1979.

Collins, John M. *U.S.–Soviet Military Balance, Concepts and Capabilities 1960–1980*. New York: McGraw-Hill, 1980.

Cotter, Donald R., et al. *The Nuclear "Balance" in Europe: Status, Trends, Implications*. Washington, D.C.: U.S. Strategic Institute, 1983.

Douglass, Joseph D., Jr. *Soviet Military Strategy in Europe*. New York: Pergamon Press, 1980.

Earle, Edward Meade, ed. *Makers of Modern Strategy*. New York: Princeton University Press, 1943.

Enthoven, Alain C., and K. Wayne Smith. *How Much Is Enough? Shaping the Defense Program, 1961–1969*. New York: Harper & Row, 1971.

Gaddis, John Lewis. *Strategies of Containment, A Critical Appraisal of Postwar American National Security Policy*. New York: Oxford University Press, 1982.

Golden, James R. *NATO Burden-Sharing, Risks and Opportunities*. New York: Praeger Publishers, 1983.

Hart, B.H. Liddell. *Strategy*. New York: Frederick A. Praeger, 1967.

Heilbrun, Otto. *Conventional Warfare in the Nuclear Age*. New York: Frederick A. Praeger, 1965.

Hunt, Kenneth. *The Alliance and Europe, Defense With Fewer Men*. London: International Institute for Strategic Studies, 1973.

Jomini, Henri. *The Art of War*. Westport: Greenwood Press.

Karanowski, Stanley M. *The German Army and NATO Strategy*. Washington, D.C.: National Defense University Press, 1982.

Karber, Phillip A. *To Lose An Arms Race: The Competition in Conventional Forces Deployed in Central Europe 1965–1980*. A paper presented at the European American Institute for Security Research, St. Paul de Vence, France, September 17, 1982.

Kaufmann, William W. *Planning Conventional Forces 1950–1980*. Washington, D.C.: The Brookings Institution, 1982.

Kissinger, Henry. *The White House Years*. Boston: Little, Brown and Company, 1979.

Leuthy, Herbert. *France Against Herself*. New York: Praeger, 1955.

Lewis, William J. *The Warsaw Pact: Arms, Doctrine and Strategy*. Washington, D.C.: Institute for Foreign Policy Analysis, 1982.

Lomov, N.A. *Scientific-Technical Progress and the Revolution in Military Affairs*. Translated and published under the auspices of the U.S. Air Force. Washington, D.C.: U.S. Government Printing Office, 1974.

Luvaas, Jay. *Frederick the Great and the Art of War*. Edited and translated by Jay Luvaas. New York: The Free Press, 1966.

Mahan, Alfred Thayer. *The Influence of Sea Power upon History, 1660–1783*. Boston: Little, Brown and Company, 1890.

Mako, William P. *U.S. Ground Forces and the Defense of Central Europe*. Washington, D.C.: The Brookings Institution, 1983.

McNamara, Robert S. *The Essence of Security*. New York: Harper & Row, 1968.

Mearsheimer, John J. *Conventional Deterrence*. Ithaca, N.Y.: Cornell University Press, 1983.

Osgood, Robert Endicott. *NATO: The Entangling Alliance*. Chicago: University of Chicago Press, 1962.

Record, Jeffrey. *Force Reductions in Europe: Starting Over*. Cambridge, Mass.: Institute for Foreign Policy Analysis, 1980.

Record, Jeffrey. *NATO's Theater Nuclear Force Modernization Program: The Real Issues*. Cambridge, Mass.: Institute for Foreign Policy Analysis, 1981.

Record, Jeffrey. *The Rapid Deployment Force and U.S. Military Intervention in the Persian Gulf*. Cambridge, Mass.: Institute for Foreign Policy Analysis, 1981.

Record, Jeffrey, and Robert J. Hanks. *U.S. Strategy at the Crossroads: Two Views*. Cambridge, Mass.: Institute for Foreign Policy Analysis, 1982.

Savkin, V. Ye. *Basic Principles of Operational Art and Tactics*. Translated and published under the auspices of the U.S. Air Force. Washington, D.C.: U.S. Government Printing Office, 1974.

Sidorenko, A.A. *The Offensive (A Soviet View)*. Translated and published under the auspices of the U.S. Air Force. Washington, D.C.: U.S. Government Printing Office, 1973.

Simpson, B. Mitchell III. *The Development of Naval Thought, Essays by Herbert Rosinski*. Newport: Naval War College Press, 1977.

Summers, Harry G. Jr. *On Strategy, A Critical Analysis of the Vietnam War*. Novato, Calif.: Presidio Press, 1982.

Sun Tzu, *The Art of War*. Translated and with an introduction by Samuel B. Griffith. New York: Oxford University Press, 1981.

Taylor, Maxwell D. *The Uncertain Trumpet*. New York: Harper Brothers, 1959.

Tucker, Robert W., and Linda Wrigley, eds. *The Atlantic Alliance and Its Critics*. New York: Praeger Publishers, 1983.

Vigor, P.H. *Soviet Blitzkrieg Theory*. New York: St. Martin's Press, 1983.

Weigley, Russell F. *History of the United States Army*. New York: Macmillan Publishing Co., Inc., 1967.

Wright, Quincy. *A Study of War*. Chicago: University of Chicago Press, 1942.

Documents

Collins, John M., et al. *Petroleum Imports from the Persian Gulf: Use of U.S. Armed Force to Ensure Supplies*. Washington, D.C.: Library of Congress Congressional Research Service, 1980.

Congressional Record, August 11, 1982.

Department of Defense Authorization for Appropriations for Fiscal Year 1981, Hearings before the Committee on Armed Services. U.S. Senate, 96th Congress, Second Session, Part 6, 1980.

Department of Defense Authorization for Appropriations for Fiscal Year 1982, Hearings before the Committee on Armed Services. U.S. Senate, 97th Congress, First Session, Part 4, 1981.

Hearings on the Military Posture and H.R. 5968. U.S. House of Representatives, 97th Congress, 2nd Session, 1982.

Iklé, Fred C. *Statement before the Senate Armed Services Committee.* February 26, 1982.

Luns, Joseph M.A.H. *NATO and Warsaw Pact Force Comparisons.* NATO, 1982.

NATO and the New Soviet Threat. Report of Senator Sam Nunn and Senator Dewey F. Bartlett to the Committee on Armed Services, U.S. Senate. Washington, D.C.: U.S. Government Printing Office, 1977.

NATO: Can the Alliance Be Saved? Report of Senator Sam Nunn to the Committee on Armed Services, U.S. Senate. Washington, D.C.: U.S. Government Printing Office, May 13, 1982.

Nixon, Richard M. *U.S. Foreign Policy for the 1970s, A New Strategy for Peace.* Washington, D.C.: U.S. Government Printing Office, 1970.

Rapid Deployment Forces: Policy and Budgetary Implications. Washington, D.C.: Congressional Budget Office, 1983.

Soviet Military Power. 2nd ed. Washington, D.C.: Department of Defense, 1983.

Testimony of General Edward C. Meyer before the Senate Armed Services Committee, February 2, 1982.

Testimony of Lt. Gen. P.X. Kelley before the Senate Armed Services Subcommittee on Sea Power and Force Projection, March 9, 1981.

United States Military Posture FY 1984. Washington, D.C.: Department of Defense, 1983.

Weinberger, Caspar W. *Annual Report to the Congress for Fiscal Year 1983.* Washington, D.C.: U.S. Government Printing Office, 1982.

Weinberger, Caspar W. *Annual Report to the Congress for Fiscal Year 1984.* Washington, D.C.: U.S. Government Printing Office, 1983.

Articles

Blacker, Coit D. "Military Forces." In Robert F. Byrnes, ed. *After Brezhnev, Sources of Soviet Conduct in the 1980s.* Bloomington: Indiana University Press, 1983.

Carter, Barry E. "Strengthening Our Conventional Defense Forces." In *Rethinking Defense and Conventional Forces.* Washington, D.C.: Center for National Policy, 1983.

Cordesman, Anthony H. "The NATO Central Region and the Balance of Uncertainty." *Armed Forces Journal* (July, 1983).

de Maiziere, Ulrich. "How Can Germany Best Be Defended?" *AEI Foreign Policy and Defense Review* 4:3/4 (March 1983).

de Rose, Francois. "Inflexible Response." *Foreign Affairs* (Spring, 1982).

Donnelly, Christopher N. "Soviet Operational Concepts in the 1980s." In *Strengthening Conventional Defense Proposals for the 1980s.* Report of the European Security Study Group. New York: St. Martin's Press, 1983.

Halloran, Richard. "New Weinberger Directive Refines Military Policy." *New York Times* (May 27, 1982).

Jones, David C. "What Is Wrong With Our Defense Establishment." *New York Times Magazine* (November 7, 1983).

Kepley, David R. "The Senate and the Great Debate of 1951." *Prologue* (Winter, 1982).

Komer, Robert W. "Future U.S. Conventional Forces: A Coalition Approach." In *Rethinking Defense and Conventional Forces.* Washington, D.C.: Center for National Policy, 1983.

Komer, Robert W. "Maritime Strategy vs. Coalition Defense." *Foreign Affairs* (Summer, 1982).

Krauss, Melvyn B. "It's Time to Change the Atlantic Alliance." *Wall Street Journal* (March 3, 1983).

Kuhn, George W.S. "Ending Defense Stagnation." In Richard N. Holwill, ed. *Agenda '83.* Washington, D.C.: The Heritage Foundation, 1982.

Nunn, Sam. "The Need to Reshape Military Strategy." Speech before the Georgetown Center for Strategic and International Studies, March 18, 1983.

"Pentagon Report to Congress Hits NATO Allies' Defense Spending." *Washington Post* (June 29, 1983).

Posen, Barry R., and Stephen Van Evera. "Defense Policy and the Reagan Administration: Departure from Containment." *International Security* (Summer, 1983).

Record, Jeffrey. "Forward Defense and Striking Deep." *Armed Forces Journal* (November, 1983).

Record, Jeffrey. "The RDF: Is the Pentagon Kidding?" *Washington Quarterly* (Summer, 1981).

Schlesinger, James R. "The Geopolitics of Energy." *Washington Quarterly* (Summer, 1979).

Schulze, Franz-Joseph. "Improving Our Conventional Defense." *AEI Foreign Policy and Defense Review* 4:3/4 (March, 1983).

Sullivan, Leonard, Jr. "Correlating National Security Strategy and Defense Investment." In W. Scott Thompson, ed. *National Security in the 1980s, From Weakness to Strength.* San Francisco: Institute for Contemporary Studies, 1980.

Sullivan, Leonard, Jr. "The Real Long-Range Defense Dilemma: Burden Sharing." *Armed Forces Journal* (October, 1981).

Turner, Stansfield, and George Thibault. "Preparing for the Unexpected: The Need for A New Military Strategy." *Foreign Affairs* (Fall, 1982).

West, Francis J., Jr. "Conventional Forces Beyond NATO." In W. Scott Thompson, ed. *National Security in the 1980s, From Weakness to Strength.* San Francisco: Institute for Contemporary Studies, 1980.

Whiting, Allen S. "Sino-American Relations: The Decade Ahead." *Orbis* (Fall, 1982).

"Will Europe help America help Europe?" *The Economist* (December 11, 1982).

Wilson, George C. "U.S. Defense Paper Cites Gap Between Rhetoric, Intentions." *Washington Post* (May 27, 1982).

INDEX

ABOUT THE AUTHOR

Jeffrey Record is a prominent expert and commentator on military affairs. Currently a Senior Fellow at the Institute for Foreign Policy Analysis and Adjunct Professor of Military History at Georgetown University, Record formerly was a member of the Brookings Institution's Defense Analysis Staff and later served for four years as Senator Sam Nunn's Legislative Assistant for National Security Affairs. Record received his Ph.D. in International Relations from the Johns Hopkins School of Advanced International Studies in 1973, and currently resides in Silver Spring, Maryland, with his wife and two sons.